D1242906

DISCOVERY & EXPLORATION

Opening Up North America, 1497–1800

Revised Edition

DISCOVERY & EXPLORATION

Opening Up North America, 1497–1800

Revised Edition

CAROLINE COX AND **KEN ALBALA**

JOHN S. BOWMAN and MAURICE ISSERMAN
General Editors

CHELSEA HOUSE
P U B L I S H E R S
An imprint of Infobase Publishing

Chelsea House
An imprint of Infobase Publishing
132 West 31st Street
New York, NY 10001

Library of Congress Cataloging-in-Publication Data
Cox, Caroline, 1954-
  Opening up North America, 1497-1800 / Caroline Cox and Ken Albala. -- Rev. ed.
      p. cm. -- (Discovery and exploration)
  Includes bibliographical references and index.
  ISBN 978-1-60413-196-3 (hardcover : acid-free paper) 1. North America--Discovery and exploration--Juvenile literature. 2. Explorers--North America--History--Juvenile literature. I. Albala, Ken, 1964- II. Title. III. Series.

  E45.C67 2009
  917.04--dc22
                              2009027794

Text design by Erika K. Arroyo
Cover design by Keith Trego
Composition by EJB Publishing Services
Cover printed by Bang Printing, Brainerd, MN
Book printed and bound by Bang Printing, Brainerd, MN
Date printed: December 2009
Printed in the United States of America

10 9 8 7 6 5 4 3 2 1

This book is printed on acid-free paper.

Contents

1

Triumph and Disappointment 1789–1793

IN JULY 1793, A YOUNG SCOT, ALEXANDER MACKENZIE, WAS LEADING a party of nine men and a friendly dog. He later wrote that they had "come in sight of the sea." That sea was the Pacific Ocean. Mackenzie's party had fulfilled the hopes of European explorers for more than two centuries. They had found a northern route across North America. Over the years, explorers and fur traders had steadily extended their knowledge of the continent's waterways farther and farther into the west. Now Mackenzie had completed the last part of the puzzle.

Mackenzie had crossed the Continental Divide and discovered a route down the western side of the Rocky Mountains and found himself gazing out at the Pacific Ocean. He had set off on the journey out of a sense of adventure and also wanted to add to his knowledge of the region. He had embarked on the journey on behalf of his fur trading company, the North West Company, in which he was a partner. He was also exploring for his nation, Great Britain. Great Britain rewarded him a few years later by making him a knight: He became Sir Alexander Mackenzie.

As Mackenzie gazed out on the Pacific, he knew there was still a lot of work to be done. The group was only at the mouth of the river they had traveled down, and he wanted to get out to the open sea. They headed out into the channel and into a strong wind. They were buffeted so much that they had to shelter in a small cove. Dangerously low on food supplies, Mackenzie and his men celebrated with a dinner of boiled porcupine. Mackenzie was anxious to find a safe spot from which he could calculate his exact latitude, so he moved the group to a small rocky island.

On that island, amid a bustle of trade with Native Peoples in furs and sea otter pelts, Mackenzie calculated their latitude. This measurement would prove to the world that his party had reached the Pacific Ocean. As the group was packing up to leave later that morning, Mackenzie decided to leave what he called a "brief memorial" of their visit. Using a mixture of bear grease and vermillion, a red dye, he wrote the following inscription on the face of a rock: "Alex Mackenzie from Canada by land 22d July 1793."

MACKENZIE'S FIRST EXPEDITION

Mackenzie had been born in Scotland in 1762 to a wealthy family. He had emigrated to North America with some relatives when he was 12 years old. Little is known about his early life. When he wrote a book of his expeditions in 1801, he was a wealthy man and publicly honored for his accomplishments, yet he said little about his childhood. However, he did reveal that he had always had "an inquisitive mind and an enterprising spirit" matched with "a body equal to the most arduous undertakings." He revealed he had been ambitious too.

Shortly after his arrival in North America, Mackenzie headed to the territory northwest of Lake Superior to enter the fur trade. He was successful and led many expeditions, steadily extending European knowledge of the continent and the scope of the fur trade. Mackenzie was sure it was possible to get to the Pacific Ocean across the continent and felt he had the skills to find the route. So he began what he called "the perilous enterprise."

This journey in 1793 was not his first attempt to reach the Pacific. The first had been in June 1789, when he led an expedition that set off down the Slave River from Fort Chipewyan on Lake Athabasca, in what is today northern Alberta, Canada. That journey resembled many earlier expeditions. It involved careful planning and gathering together all the most recent information from others who traveled in the region, namely Europeans and Native Americans. Just as with other exploring parties, Mackenzie's would trade for furs as it went and pay for the costs of the expedition with the profits.

Mackenzie's party included the Native American wives of two French Canadian traders. It also included the Chipewyan leader, Nestabeck. Nestabeck's two wives and other young Native American men also

Alexander Mackenzie attempted to reach the Pacific Ocean many times before succeeding in 1793. He is credited with extending European knowledge of North America and the fur trade.

joined the group. Guides and interpreters would have to be recruited along the way. Nestabeck's role was critical, although they were traveling into territory unknown to him. While Mackenzie would do what he could, much depended on Nestabeck, whom Mackenzie described in his account as "a principal leader of his countrymen."

The journey confronted them with moments of great hope and great fear, as well as delays, frustrations, and lots of hard work. At the high latitudes in which they were traveling, summer comes late. Even though it was June, the ice was just breaking up on the rivers and lakes as they headed to the Great Slave Lake. European traders who had visited that lake before had heard from Native Peoples of a great river that flowed from the lake. That was what Mackenzie was hoping to find. It took a long time, and even their local guide from the Yellowknife people got lost. Nestabeck was furious with the guide and, according to Mackenzie, flew into "a great passion." After searching through inlets, coves, ice, and rocks, they eventually found the entrance to the great river. On maps today, it bears Mackenzie's name. At more than 1,100 miles (1,770 kilometers) long and often more than half a mile (0.8 km) wide, it is one of the great rivers of the world.

Unfortunately, the river did not lead to the Pacific. High mountains were always to their west, and there was no sign of a break in them through which the river might wind. Ice was forming on the river at night even though it was July and information they picked up from local people was not encouraging. They had met small groups of Slave and Dogrib people, who had been nervous as the strangers approached; however, Nestabeck found some among them who spoke Chipewyan and was able to smooth the path. The sea, they said, was a long way off and filled with danger. This news made Mackenzie's own party anxious to turn back; nevertheless, once they had a local guide with them, they agreed to press on.

Still, the river flowed northwest and made no sharp turn to the west. They traveled through a great gorge where the river spilled out into a broad channel with many islands. Mackenzie's calculations showed they were at latitude 67°N (67 degrees north). There was ice on the riverbanks, and the weather was getting steadily colder. Mackenzie again had to talk his party into pressing onward. They met the Inuit peoples of the Arctic region, whom Mackenzie called "Eskmeaux," who told them they were not far from the sea. A few days later, when Mackenzie and Nestabeck climbed a hill for a better view, they looked down on a huge body of water filled with ice floes. The ice and the whales they later saw convinced Mackenzie they were at the Arctic Sea. (They were at what is today called the Beaufort Sea.)

Mackenzie was disappointed. He had mapped a great river to an ocean. He made detailed notes about the landscape, the peoples he

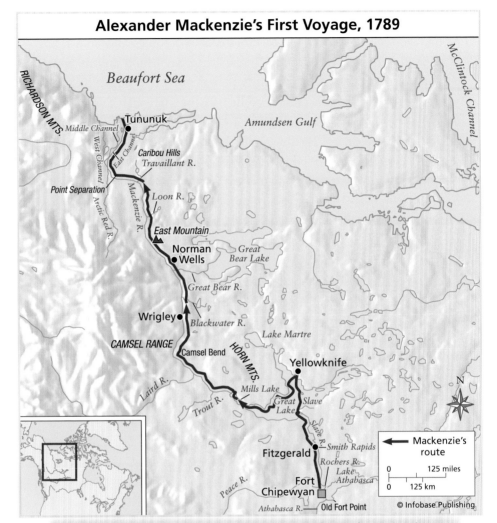

Alexander Mackenzie's First Voyage, 1789

RICHARDSON MTS.

Beaufort Sea

Middle Channel

West Channel

East Channel

Tununuk

Amundsen Gulf

McClintock Channel

Caribou Hills
Travaillant R.

Point Separation

Mackenzie R.

Arctic Red R.

Loon R.

East Mountain

Norman
Wells

Great
Bear Lake

Great Bear R.

Wrigley
Blackwater R.

Lake Martre

CAMSEL RANGE

Camsel Bend

HORN MTS.

Yellowknife

Laird R.

Trout R.

Mills Lake

Great Slave
Lake

Slave R.

Fitzgerald

Smith Rapids

Rochers R.

Lake
Athabasca

Peace R.

Fort
Chipewyan

Athabasca R.

Old Fort Point

N

⬅ Mackenzie's
route

0   125 miles

0   125 km

© Infobase Publishing

In hopes of finding a northwest passage through the Rocky Mountains to the Pacific Ocean, Alexander Mackenzie reached the Beaufort Sea, the part of the Arctic Ocean located above northwest Canada. Disappointment River is now named Mackenzie River after the explorer.

encountered, and their way of life. He had opened the door to future traders, advancing the understanding of the great waterways of the sub-Arctic. When they returned to Fort Chipewyan, the group had traveled a journey of nearly 3,000 miles (4,828 km) without mishap. But he had not found the route to the Pacific.

MACKENZIE'S SECOND EXPEDITION

Nonetheless, he was even more certain that such a route existed. In 1792, after visiting England to improve his skills in navigation and mapping and to acquire some new instruments, he was ready to try again. Now 30 years old, Mackenzie was convinced he was the man with the skill and experience to lead another expedition to find it. His next attempt would take place in two stages. The first would take his expedition high into the Rockies. There an advance party already would have prepared the ground to build a fort. The fort would be the expedition's winter quarters and a future trading post. After waiting through the winter, trading and preparing equipment, the second stage of the expedition would take place as soon as the snow melted the following spring. Then the men would cross the Rockies and try to find a river that would lead to the Pacific.

Mackenzie knew that having a good team was critical to success. Earlier experience taught him to keep the expedition as lean and efficient as possible. On the second stage of the expedition, he only took nine men with him. Among these, the leading figure was the 22-year-old Alexander MacKay, a seasoned backwoodsman. Mackenzie had particularly wanted MacKay to join the group. MacKay had been born in New York to a Loyalist family, just before the American Revolution. (Loyalists were those who stayed loyal to the British during the Revolution.) The MacKay family and many other Loyalists left the United States during and after the war and went to live in what was known as Upper Canada, now Ontario. As a young man, MacKay went west to enter the fur trade. Now, on Mackenzie's expedition, MacKay quickly became Mackenzie's right-hand man. Mackenzie always referred to MacKay as his assistant, and it was frequently MacKay's assistance that was critical to success in difficult situations. Of the other team members, two men, Joseph Landry and Charles Ducette, had traveled with Mackenzie on the 1789 expedition to the Arctic. Of the remaining six men in the party, four men were French Canadian. The final two that later joined the party were young Native American men.

One thing they all had in common was lots of experience as canoe men on the rivers of the West. This experience was critical. Much of the journey would involve paddling on rivers and the pace would be grueling. The group was traveling in a specially built, lightweight canoe that was 25 feet (7.6 meters) long and just under 5 feet (1.5 m) at its widest part. The weight of the canoe was important, because the trip would involve many portages. A portage is when the canoe and all the baggage and supplies have to be carried across land. Therefore, Mackenzie wanted a canoe that two men could carry "three or four miles [4 or 6 km] without resting." No other men could be spared for the task because they would be carrying more than 3,000 pounds (1,360 kilograms) of supplies.

THE EXPEDITION SETS OFF

On October 10, 1792, the expedition (at this time probably about 12 men total) set off on the first stage from Fort Chipewyan on Lake Athabasca.

BIRCH-BARK CANOES

Canoes were the main means of transportation on the rivers and streams of North America when the first Europeans arrived. European explorers and fur traders quickly copied Native American construction techniques. Materials varied from region to region, but in northern latitudes, travelers used birch-bark canoes. The frame of the canoe was usually made of white cedar. Only its outer skin was birch bark. The roots of a spruce tree were used to sew the sections of bark together. The resin of the spruce was used to glue it to make it watertight.

The Native Americans had developed a technique whereby they could take the bark from a birch tree without killing the tree. They made a vertical cut down the length of the tree trunk, but they cut through only the outer bark. The outer bark could then be peeled off in huge strips, leaving the inner layer, the living layer, intact and the tree alive. A single strip of bark could be up to 2.5 feet (0.7 m) wide and up to 15 feet (4.5 m) long. Pieces this size meant that less stitching and gluing needed to be done, and they made the canoe stronger. An experienced canoe builder could look at a tree and tell where the thickest bark was. This thick bark was best for the bottom of the canoe, where it would bear the most weight. The largest canoes used by the fur traders were 36 feet (10.9 m) in length and could carry a load up to 6,000 pounds (2,721 kg).

They followed the Peace River to the west. By late October, they reached the fork of the Peace and Smoky rivers, on the eastern side of the Rocky Mountains. Here they met up with the advance party and completed building what they called Fort Fork, where they spent the winter. Even though they now needed to work on the construction of their winter shelter, the men probably were glad to do work other than paddling canoes. Mackenzie wrote that they had been exhausted when they arrived, which was hardly surprising. Not only had they just completed the first stage of this journey, most of the men who were with him had also, earlier that year, taken furs from Fort Chipewyan to Rainy Lake, just west of Lake Superior, and come back with supplies. All these miles would have been logged in canoes on the rivers and lakes that were the highways of the fur trade.

During the winter at Fort Fork, Mackenzie was restless and anxious to be on his way. The wait was profitable, however, because he spent it trading with Native Americans. As soon as spring came, he sent a canoe laden with furs back to Fort Chipewyan. The profits on these furs would help pay for the expedition.

The group set off in May 1793, as soon as the ground thawed. It was only just as they were leaving that Mackenzie was able to recruit the two young Native American men to come with them. He had trouble convincing the young men to come, as they had been worried about the journey, but Mackenzie managed to persuade them. He did not need them as guides; they did not know the terrain where the party was going either. Nevertheless, Mackenzie needed them to help recruit guides as they went along. He also needed them as hunters to add to the party's food supply and to be interpreters. Indeed, as Mackenzie observed, "Without Indians I have very little hopes of succeeding."

The second stage of the expedition traveled along the Peace River with the hope of finding a pass through the Rocky Mountains. Then, on the western side, they hoped to find a river that would take them to the Pacific. They had to portage many times around rapids and falls. With the help of the Sekani people, who provided advice and a guide, they were able to portage over a series of mountain lakes.

Finally, they crossed the Continental Divide. This point separates the eastward-flowing watershed from the westward, Pacific-flowing one. They followed the MacGregor River and briefly the Fraser River

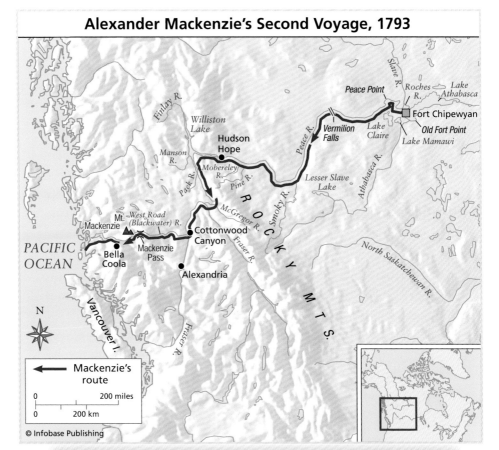

Alexander Mackenzie's Second Voyage, 1793

Four years after his first expedition, Mackenzie was given another chance to find a way to reach the Pacific Ocean. He and his crew found the Northwest Passage in 1793, although it was too difficult a passage for general travel.

before being forced by its raging waters to seek an alternate route over land. Finally, they reached the Bella Coola River, which took them to the coast. On their journey, they met many different groups of Native Americans, heard unfamiliar languages, and observed different cultures. Sometimes they feared for their lives from the people they met or from the rivers, but they arrived at the coast safely. Satisfied with their accomplishments, the group now began its difficult return journey over the Rockies. They arrived back at Fort Fork on August 24.

To round out the expedition, they had taken along a dog, which Mackenzie never named in his account but simply referred to as "our dog." The dog had traveled with them until they were within a few days' journey of the coast. Then, during a stay in a village, it wandered off, and they were forced to go on without it. This, Mackenzie remembered, was "a circumstance of no small regret to me." On their journey home they came near that village again. They found the dog, confused and hungry. Mackenzie remembered they all felt as if they had "found a lost friend" and "our dog" rejoined them. Men and beast made it safely home to Fort Chipewyan, having become the first known party to cross the continent north of Mexico.

Mackenzie had shown that a well-chosen group, good preparation, the support of Native Americans, and skilled leadership were the keys to success in exploration. Mackenzie and others who had gone before him were motivated by a desire for adventure and by financial ambition. Their personal ambitions were the same as those of merchants and traders and of nations and kings. It had been nearly 300 years since Europeans had landed on the coast of northeastern North America. When John Cabot first arrived on the shores of Newfoundland in 1497, little did he know that he would be initiating a quest that would involve several European nations and hundreds of Native American peoples. Nor could he have known that it would take three centuries, countless disasters, battles, and losses of life to finally reach the Pacific.

2

Exploration and Empire 1497–1536

ON THE FIFTH DAY OF MARCH 1496, KING HENRY VII OF ENGLAND personally witnessed scribes carefully draft a wide horizontal document in Latin bearing the name "John Kabotto." This official document was called letters patent. It granted exclusive rights to conquer and trade with any newly discovered land. John Cabot, as he has come to be known, was given control over a route across the North Atlantic Ocean all the way to China. Henry VII may have been thinking only about all the gold coins he would be counting after England controlled the spice trade with Asia. With these letters patent, however, he had started England on the path of exploration and empire building.

The great era of European exploration began well before 1496 or even 1492, and it could have happened much earlier had Asian explorers been motivated to reach Europe and the Americas. But certain factors made it easier for Europeans to make the journey: the development of seaworthy ships and favorable currents; improved navigational techniques; and, most important, money, which was provided by powerful kings or private investors who were granted charters and monopolies. There also were many reasons for Europeans to set forth. Profit was usually the most obvious motive, but explorers often had a desire to gain new converts to Christianity, as well as a lust for personal glory. Kings and queens became interested in exploration so they could finance their growing administrations and wage war, and rulers wanted to cash in on the anticipated riches of new lands before their neighbors. So the development of the nation-state, a country with well-defined borders and a unified administration, was itself a crucial factor in European exploration.

What may seem surprising is that exploration was rarely a goal in itself. What Europeans of the fifteenth century wanted to reach first and foremost was Asia. From India and the Moluccas—the island group also known as the Spice Islands that are today part of Indonesia—came rare and exotic spices, perfumes, and dyes. These were the ultimate luxury goods of the late Middle Ages. Only the wealthiest people could afford to pay the enormously inflated costs of transport and passage through the hands of dozens of middlemen. A cargo of cloves, for example, would travel from the Spice Islands either overland via the silk route from China or in small boats called dhows by Arab merchants around India. They would go to ports in the Middle East such as Aleppo, Syria; Beirut, Lebanon; or Alexandria, Egypt, and from there they would be picked up by Venetian middlemen, who would in turn pass them on to the rest of Europe. Imported spices such as pepper, cinnamon, cloves, ginger, and nutmeg were extraordinarily expensive and thus perfect status symbols. Anyone who could afford to heap huge amounts of spice on his or her food must have been fantastically rich. Spices were even believed to have wonderful medicinal virtues. It is no wonder that the cost of spices, and the profit made by merchants who supplied them, was astronomical.

Although it had stiff competition through much of the Middle Ages, by the fifteenth century Venice, at the top of the Adriatic Sea, had almost complete control of the spice trade. Its only real competitors were the merchants of Genoa, on the other side of Italy. The success of the Venetians owed a lot to the way they had set up their mercantile empire. The Republic of Venice not only sponsored the construction of galleys in a huge arsenal, they also protected shipping to the eastern Mediterranean by conquering territory along the Dalmatian coast of the Adriatic Sea all the way to Greece as well as the islands of Crete and Cyprus. By controlling many ports along the trade route, they could easily pick up food and fresh water or reinforcements, if necessary. The galleys themselves were huge flat-bottomed vessels rigged with square sails and manned with oars for maneuverability and mobility in case the wind gave out. They had been used for centuries, and although they sometimes were taken into the Atlantic, they were not particularly

Today spices are used mainly for flavoring foods. In the past, spices were the most luxurious products available, used only by the wealthy. They were used as medicine, to mask the odor of decayed food, and to embalm the bodies of the nobles. In just two centuries after the European and Middle Eastern monopoly on the spice trade, spices that were once limited to tiny islands were being grown around the world in large quantities.

stable among large waves, strong wind gusts, and ocean currents. They were ideally suited for the Mediterranean, though.

Their position on the Atlantic demanded that the Portuguese develop seaworthy ships. In the course of the latter Middle Ages they used the caravel—a small tublike vessel with high fore and aft structures known as castles, three masts, and lateen, or triangular, sails good for sailing into the wind. They later built larger ships such as the *naõ*, which had a combination of square and triangular rigging and several sails per mast, which added to maneuverability. Portugal's Prince Henry, although he himself did not sail on any voyage, earned the name "the Navigator" because he sponsored voyages down the coast of West Africa. The Portuguese also had a long tradition of mapmaking, using what is called a portolan (port guide), a chart to measure distance and direction between ports. From the west coast of Africa, they picked up gold, ivory, and slaves, all of which fetched high prices in Europe. The Portuguese also decided to use these slaves in a way that foreshadowed developments of the next century. On islands such as Madeira, the Portuguese possession off the northwest coast of Africa, they used slave labor to grow and process sugar cane, which was then classified among the most sought-after of spices. In other words, they cut out the middlemen who supplied sugar from Asia by growing it themselves. It then occurred to them that they might find a direct route to Asia by going around the tip of Africa and from there travel directly to India, Indonesia, and China.

The only major difficulty with this plan was that the Atlantic currents and winds in the Northern Hemisphere run clockwise, which was fine as long as one was heading for the ivory or gold coast of Africa and down to the equator. But in the Southern Hemisphere the currents run counterclockwise. This meant that a ship hugging the coastline would be pushed northward. It took a great leap of imagination and courage to follow the currents far out into the ocean—toward modern-day Brazil, which they would later bump into—in order to come back to South Africa. It was Bartolomeu Dias who first performed this feat in 1488. He reached the tip of South Africa, which he named the Cape of Storms but then was later renamed the Cape of Good Hope by the king of Portugal in expectation of finding a direct sea route to India.

COMPETITION FOR NEW LANDS

News of Dias's feat set in motion the European competition for new lands. If the Portuguese could establish a direct trade route to Asia, they could effectively cut out all competition, import a much greater supply of spices, and control prices. This is precisely what they did in the next few decades after Vasco da Gama rounded the cape and landed in Calicut on the west coast of India in 1498. The Portuguese subsequently established posts in Goa (India), Malacca, elsewhere in Indonesia, and as far as China and Japan, building *feitoria,* or trading posts, much as the Venetians had done. This direct trade route did not enable the Portuguese to immediately replace the Venetians as the premier spice merchants of Europe (that would take another century), but by the 1480s the race was under way.

Only one among several figures in this contest was Genoese merchant-mariner Christopher Columbus. He first took his proposal to discover a western route to Asia to the Portuguese. He also sent his brother Bartholomew to seek the support of England and France, which were probably good choices, considering these were wealthy nations. In the end, it was Spain that accepted his plan to find this alternate route to Asia. For the moment, however, the rulers of Spain, Ferdinand of Aragon and Isabella of Castile, were busy with their own problems of unifying their nation. They accomplished this with the conquest of the last remaining outpost of Muslim control, the kingdom of Granada, and with the expulsion of the Jews. Both these events took place in 1492, and only then could Ferdinand and Isabella turn their attention to overseas voyages.

Their initial unwillingness to support Columbus had nothing to do with their ideas about the shape of Earth. Most Europeans at that time knew that Earth is a sphere, something that had been accepted as fact since antiquity. What the king and queen feared was the great distance and unlikely chances of success. In the end, what prompted them to finance him was precisely the fear of a Portuguese monopoly and the possibility of becoming a poor neighbor. Another factor is that Spain, or more properly Ferdinand of Aragon, had ambitions to control the entire western Mediterranean. He had a serious claim to Sicily and the kingdom of Naples. By the 1490s, this would drag Spain into a major war against France, fought mostly on Italian soil, which would last through half of the next century. What might have ended as a brief episode was extended into a major program of exploration and conquest. This was driven to a large extent by the Spanish Crown's constant need for money to pay for this and other wars. To ensure this income, they demanded 20 percent of all profits from overseas voyages.

The great irony of Columbus's achievement, the so-called discovery of America, is that he was convinced until the day he died that he had found a route to Asia. (He did, however, realize that he had discovered what he himself called "an other world.") His journals record his almost desperate search for spices and gold and his assurance to the Spanish monarchs that he had found what he was seeking. Neither he nor they could even begin to suspect the sheer size and riches of the New World that he had come upon. Columbus's discovery was publicized through-out Europe almost immediately after his return to Spain, and the fact that he returned with Native Americans, parrots, and promises of gold only made other nations all the more envious and soon fearful that Spain would become the most powerful nation in Europe.

In particular, Spain's advantage did not escape the attention of two other emerging nation-states, England and France, and it was at this point that North America finally entered the picture. Portugal con-trolled the eastward route to Asia. Spain, following Columbus's voyages, hoped to dominate the westerly route. Their claims to these two routes were formally sanctioned in 1494 by the Treaty of Tordesillas (named after a city in northern Spain), by which Pope Alexander VI basically divided the known world between the two powers. But perhaps there was another route to Asia, a passage via the northwest, far from Spanish control. The English and French were perfectly positioned to attempt to find it. By 1505, Basque and French fishermen were already sailing as far as the shores of North America in search of cod, which, when salted and dried, was an important food throughout Europe. None of these fishermen had established permanent settlements or even charted their course, but it was not inconceivable to do so.

JOHN CABOT'S VOYAGES

The merchants of Bristol, on the southwest coast of England, had begun to send out voyages into the Atlantic. They hoped to find islands that might provide a base for further exploration and trade. It was to them that the Italian merchant Giovanni Cabotto (who became "John Kabo-tto" in the letters patent referred to at the beginning of this chapter) turned with the idea of plotting his own route to Asia across a north-west passage. News had reached Europe that Columbus had sailed west to islands adjacent to Asia. John Cabot, as he came to be called in Eng-land, thought he could match Columbus's discovery. Cabot figured that the distance across the Atlantic would be much shorter at a northerly latitude than Columbus's route.

News of Cabot's plan reached England's King Henry VII, himself a shrewd engineer of a centralized monarchy, who had managed to put his own country's finances in order. Expansion of English trade and the potential customs duties due the Crown were certainly a prime reason he decided to give Cabot an official charter. The king would

John Cabot received funding from England's King Henry VII to find a northwest passage to the Indies at a northerly latitude rather than around the middle of Earth. Above, Cabot receives the letters patent from King Henry VII to sail in search of new lands.

take 20 percent of Cabot's profits. In return, Cabot could govern whatever lands he found.

Cabot himself, though probably born in Genoa, gained his experience working for Venice in the lucrative spice trade to Mecca in Arabia. Cabot should have known where spices came from, but he believed they grew in northern Asia, a fatal mistake as it turned out.

With letters patent granting exclusive rights, Cabot set out from Bristol in May 1497. He had one small boat, the *Mathew*, of about 50 tuns (a tun was a large barrel, so 50 tuns meant a ship could hold 50 large barrels) and a tiny crew of 18. In only 35 days, Cabot made the voyage to North America, landing on June 24, 1497. There is really no way of knowing exactly where Cabot landed, and there is still a great deal of dispute among historians whether he landed on Cape Breton Island (off of mainland Nova Scotia, Canada) or way to the north on the tip of Newfoundland (off of Canada's eastern coast). Wherever he actually landed, he sailed around for about a month, presumably charting the waters in preparation for his next visit. Although Cabot and his crew did not meet any Native Americans, they did find evidence of them. Cabot did not waste time exploring the land or searching for inhabitants, but he did recognize that this was a new land. He believed he was somewhere east of Japan, or Cipangu, as it was called at that time. The region came to be called New Isle or Newfoundland, and it was formally claimed for England. If Cabot did actually touch on the mainland of North America, then this was the first recorded voyage to do so since the Vikings and predates even Columbus's setting foot on the mainland of South America.

Upon his return to England, Cabot could not dazzle the court with gold, slaves, or parrots as had his competitor Columbus to the Spanish court. But Cabot's story caused a brief sensation. He was seen swaggering about the streets of Bristol as a hero. Henry VII even granted him an allowance. Plans were laid for a second voyage to set up a permanent colony and a trading post—much along the same lines as the Portuguese were building on the other side of Asia. A dispatch to the duke of Milan from his envoy in London, Raimondo di Soncino, one of the only pieces of contemporary evidence regarding these events, even claims that Henry intended to "give him all the malefactors to go to that country and form a colony." In other words, this was to be a penal colony to dump off prisoners, presumably the only people willing to go. Whoever populated it, Cabot was firmly convinced that, with a trading post, he could make England a major competitor in the spice trade. By gaining direct access to the wealth of Asia, London would become, as Soncino claimed, "a greater depot of spices . . . than there is in Alexandria."

Cabot's second voyage was well outfitted. His five ships carried a year's worth of supplies and about 200 men. One of the ships actually had to turn around quickly for repairs. The remaining four ships were never heard from again. There is also still a lot of controversy over what became of Cabot. It is thought that Cabot got as far as Chesapeake Bay (which stretches from Maryland to Virginia) on this voyage. Some people suggest that he even may have returned home. Chances are that he was either lost at sea or remained in America.

CHANGING ROLES AND GOALS

The race across the North Atlantic was taken up by John Cabot's son Sebastian. Although there is no certain evidence that he accompanied his father on any of his voyages, Sebastian and his brothers were named in the original letters patent. Sebastian was given two ships by the Bristol merchants in 1508 or 1509, again to find a northwest route to Asia. He probably knew by this point that the New World was not part of Asia, but thought there still might be a way to sail through. Searching any major waterway, he probably entered what is now Hudson Strait, north of Labrador (in Atlantic Canada), but after finding ice, was forced to turn around. He may have sailed as far south as Delaware Bay. According to his own account, he went as far as Florida. None of these waterways, of course, proved to be the passage to Asia.

These voyages made no money for England, and the country quickly got out of the spice trade. The next English king, Henry VIII, had no interest in overseas voyages. He was more interested in reviving ancient English claims to the kingdom of France and subduing the Scots. He also was seriously preoccupied with his own dynastic and religious problems for much of his reign. So while his neighbors were busy building empires, he was dealing with problems within England. The English stayed out of the race for new lands until the middle of the sixteenth century. Sebastian Cabot left to serve the Crown of Spain and returned only after Henry's death in the late 1540s, this time to seek a northeast passage to Asia across the top of Russia.

THE LAND OF CODFISH

Explorers had found no spices in the Americas. They did, however, learn that North Atlantic waters were filled with cod and its coasts were covered in timber. Soon Portuguese, Spanish, and French sailors visited the shores of the Grand Banks of Newfoundland, returning with enough fish to warrant taxation by their respective rulers. As Cabot had claimed, one need only drop a bucket into the water and it would be filled with fish.

Cod was a staple in the European diet. In some areas it was salted as bacalao. In others it was dried as stockfish. During the period of Lent (in Christian tradition, the 40 days leading up to Easter), people were not allowed to eat meat, and cod provided an affordable form of sustenance. Fishing did not provide the great wealth produced by the spice trade, but it was lucrative nonetheless. It would at least keep North America on the minds of Europeans for some time to come. By the following decade, France would be the next major competitor in the race to chart the waters and territory of North America.

The first known voyages of Frenchmen to Newfoundland took place between 1504 and 1508. At that time these people identified themselves as either Normans or Bretons—that is, inhabitants of Normandy or Brittany—or Basques, inhabitants of the region along the border of France and Spain, rather than French. These were not specifically voyages of exploration. Their primary goal was to catch codfish, a trade in which the Bretons, as well as the Basques, were well accomplished. These men did not describe the geography or attempt to chart the shores they encountered. Even if they had done so for their own personal use, they probably would not have published such information for fear of revealing to competitors the location of the best fishing banks.

Well into the sixteenth century and long after Christopher Columbus, there was still nothing approaching accurate geographical knowledge of the New World in the Western Hemisphere. Pictured on the maps were mythical places such as Brasil, Antilia, and the Fortunate Isles, or Hesperides. These places were dreamed up by medieval chroniclers or were mentioned centuries before by ancient authorities. It is no wonder that such places still figured prominently in the planning of overseas ventures, especially when explorers sought out the as-yet-uncharted shores of North America in search of a westerly passage to Asia.

THE VOYAGE OF VERRAZANO

Finding a direct route to Asia was the motivation for the expeditions led by Giovanni da Verrazano. An Italian by birth, he was given the finest education available in Florence at a time when it was the cultural center. His family had a castle in the hills south of Florence, and it is supposed that Verrazano was born there around 1485. Like his colleagues, he was lured to France by business opportunities and the dazzling court of Francis I. At the time, France was one of the most powerful and wealthy nation-states in Europe. Francis had been mostly preoccupied with wars in Italy against Charles V, king of Spain and Holy Roman Emperor, but by 1523 Francis was intent on profiting from trade with Asia. He hired Verrazano, then living in the French port town of Dieppe and experienced in the Middle East spice trade, to find the westerly passage. Francis provided a ship, and a group of Florentine silk merchants living in France helped pay for the voyage. They were looking for a source for cheap raw silk. Again, the ultimate goal was reaching Asia.

Verrazano had more accurate geographical knowledge than his English and Portuguese predecessors. Although the North American coast remained unexplored, the existence of a separate ocean, the Pacific, had been known since Vasco Núñez de Balboa crossed the Isthmus of Panama in 1513. The existence of a passage connecting the Atlantic and Pacific oceans also was reconfirmed by reports of Ferdinand Magellan's rounding the southernmost tip of South America in 1519. Magellan himself never made it home, but the sparse remains of Magellan's crew, led by Sebastian Elcano on one remaining ship, did bring back to Spain a huge load of cloves in 1522. This proved once and for all that one could sail west to reach the riches of the Spice Islands, as the East Indies were then known.

Verrazano's voyage began in January 1524. He sailed aboard a single ship, *La Dauphine*, from Dieppe. Verrazano crossed the Atlantic with 50 men and supplies for 8 months, as well as munitions in the event of hostile encounters. Verrazano made the crossing far to the north of typical Spanish routes and, thus, landed on the shores of North America at

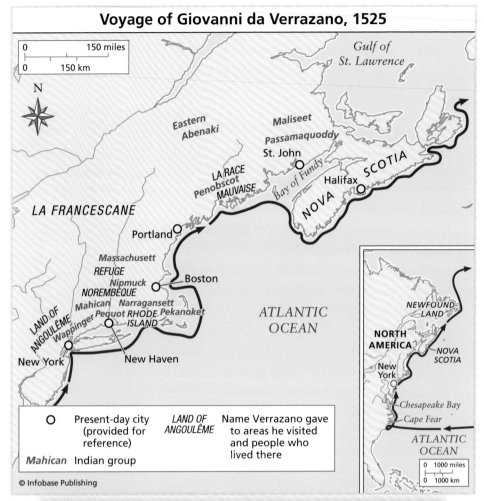

Voyage of Giovanni da Verrazano, 1525

In 1524, Giovanni da Verrazano was sent by King Francis to the Americas in search of a passageway to China. Verrazano explored the east coast of North America between South Carolina and Canada's Newfoundland.

34°N latitude, somewhere near Cape Fear at the lowest point of present-day North Carolina. As he gazed over the outer banks toward Pamlico Sound without seeing land on the other side, he believed he was looking at the Pacific Ocean. He thought this thin strip of land (from Cape Lookout to Cape Hatteras and all the way up to Virginia) was actually an isthmus like the one Balboa crossed in Panama. For many years navigators and mapmakers drew the same conclusion.

Although no logbook survives detailing these discoveries, Verrazano's remarkable letter to Francis I describes North America and his interaction with the Native populations. His letter would color European ideas of Native Americans for decades to come. In describing the natural landscape, Verrazano wrote:

> *The seashore is completely covered with sand 15 feet [4.5 meters] deep, which rises in the form of small hills about fifty paces wide. After climbing farther, we found other streams and inlets from the sea which come in by several mouths, and follow the ins and outs of the shoreline. Nearby we could see a stretch of country much higher than the sandy shore, with many beautiful fields full of great forests, some sparse and some dense; and the trees have so many colors, and are so beautiful and delightful that they defy description. . . . And these trees emit a sweet fragrance over a large area. . . . We think that they belong to the Orient by virtue of the surroundings, and that they are not without some kind of narcotic or aromatic liquor. There are other riches, like gold, which ground of such a color usually denotes. There is an abundance of animals, stags, deer, hares; and also of lakes and pools of running water with various types of bird, perfect for the delights and pleasures of the hunt.*

Verrazano chose his words carefully to keep the king interested in his explorations. Not only did he promise wealth and spices that could adorn the meals Francis served, but he seemed to offer a potential playground much like the Loire Valley where Francis had his châteaux, and beautiful parks and animals to hunt, not to mention gorgeous weather. The mid-Atlantic coastal region was beautiful. It is perhaps not surprising that today much of this very ground is covered with resorts and golf courses.

Proceeding up the coast, Verrazano appears to have missed the Chesapeake and Delaware bays. He did explore what is now the harbor of New York (hence the name of the Verrazano-Narrows Bridge, which spans the bay from Staten Island to Brooklyn today). Not until the early 1600s would another explorer set eyes on the mouth of the

Hudson and what would later become Manhattan. Verrazano named the region the Land of Angoulême in tribute to Francis's having been count of Angoulême before he became king. Why he did not proceed up

SAILORS' DIETS

The seaman's diet was coarse and dull, consisting almost entirely of dried provisions. Hardtack—biscuits consisting of little more than flour and water—were the universal staple. Salted beef, pickled beef or pork, stockfish (dried cod), or herring, perhaps beans, and wine or beer were the usual supplement to the hardtack. Europeans' ships were also usually provisioned with olive oil. Some ships carried other foods. Englishman Hugh Plat published a pamphlet in 1607 entitled *Certaine Philosophical Preparations of Foode and Beverage for Sea-men,* which recommended dried macaroni. Apparently he furnished Elizabethan privateers Francis Drake and John Hawkins with it. Physicians frequently recommended garlic for sailors, for they believed it would act as a preservative against eating foul meats and smelling bilge water. Lemons, although not standard issue until the eighteenth century, were also sometimes carried onboard to prevent scurvy. Fresh vegetables were almost unheard of as rations.

Most ships carried along live animals, usually pigs or chickens, that would be slaughtered and cooked onboard. One can easily imagine not only the difficulty but also the extraordinary danger of cooking with open flame on a wooden ship rigged with rope soaked in pitch, a flammable tar. At sea, the sailors' diets could be supplemented by fresh fish. Naturally one of the first things the crew would do when reaching land was to hunt for fresh game. Perhaps most important of all, though, was fresh water, which was needed to prevent dehydration at sea but also to soak the hardtack. A voyage whose water had gone bad was in grave peril. Even still, the sailors would not have begun drinking water until the beer or wine ran out, which must have happened frequently given the gallon of beer each seaman enjoyed every day.

the Hudson as a candidate for his passage is not known, though it seems he feared navigating beyond the bay in bad weather.

Verrazano then sailed along the south shore of Long Island. He explored Block Island (which he called Aloysia after French queen Louise) and Rhode Island (it reminded him of the island of Rhodes off of Greece). Here, his crew rested and made contact with Native Americans. He describes Native Americans as a happy, unspoiled people living in a Golden Age. This is what he had to say in his letter about one tribe:

> These people are the most beautiful and have the most civil customs that we have found on this voyage. They are taller than we are; they are a bronze color, some tending more toward whiteness, others to a tawny color; the face is clear-cut; the hair is long and black, and they take great pains to decorate it; the eyes are black and alert, and their manner is sweet and gentle, very like the manner of the ancients. I shall not speak to Your Majesty of the other parts of the body, since they have all the proportions belonging to any well-built man. Their women are just as shapely and beautiful, very gracious of attractive manner and pleasant appearance.

The very fact that the Native Americans did not value gold but preferred bells and other trinkets made Verrazano believe that he could easily take whatever gold he might find. He also thought that these were a simple people unspoiled by the trappings of corrupt civilization. They apparently were unimpressed with European weapons as well. They freely gave away whatever they had, seemingly unconcerned with material possessions. Verrazano's description sounds very much like those of classical authorities on the mythical Golden Age and, not coincidentally, like that of English scholar Thomas More in his depiction of the fictional land of Utopia.

In his progress to the north, Verrazano gave a detailed description of Narragansett Bay and may have journeyed as far as Newfoundland. He then returned to France in July 1524. The significance of these discoveries was not only that they filled in the gap between Spanish discoveries to the south and English and Portuguese discoveries to the north, but

that they also helped prove that North America was a separate continent from Asia. Verrazano named the land La Francescane. It would
soon appear on maps as New France.

Verrazano probably would have followed up this voyage with another
had not Francis needed ships to protect northern ports from a supposed
English invasion. That the king was himself taken prisoner by the Spanish at the battle of Pavia in 1525 only delayed any further exploration
for the next few years. Verrazano did eventually make other voyages.
In 1527, he went to Brazil and returned with a hefty cargo of dyewood.
And, in 1528, he went with his brother Girolamo to Florida, the Baha-
mas, and the Lesser Antilles. It was there that he met his untimely end.
On what is now the Island of Guadaloupe, he was captured by Native
Peoples. Verrazano was killed and eaten while his brother and other
crew members looked on in horror.

GOMES AND NEW ENGLAND

At about the same time as Verrazano's voyage, a Spanish expedition
was planned to find the Northwest Passage. This one was led by Este-
vão Gomes, a Portuguese navigator working for Spain. In 1523, he was
ordered to explore Eastern Cathay (China), then to sail as far as the
Moluccas in the East Indies. There he should find gold, silver, spices,
and medicinal drugs. He was also told in no uncertain terms not to
encroach on the possessions of the king of Portugal, located on the
eastern side of the demarcation line set out in the Treaty of Tordesillas
(1494), although exactly what islands that would entitle him to exploit
was not entirely clear.

Because a new caravel had to be built for this voyage, the expedition
did not get underway until September 1524, a few months after Verrazano had returned. Gomes covered much of the same ground as Verrazano, although it is still a matter of debate whether he sailed southward
from Newfoundland or northward from Florida. He explored the region
around Cape Cod (which he called San Pedro) and as far north as the
Penobscot River in Maine (which he called Río de los Gamos, or Deer
River), but naturally found no passage to Asia. In August 1525, Gomes did,
however, return with 58 Algonquian Indians taken as slaves. No doubt,
he did not want to return to Spain empty-handed. Navigators would continue to search for the Northwest Passage through the next century.

EARLY ENGLISH VOYAGERS

In 1527, England's John Rut led one final attempt to seek out a north-west passage. Robert Thorne, a Bristol merchant, initiated the voyage. He understood that the distance to Asia would be much shorter this way than the route taken by the Spanish and Portuguese. Thorne also understood that the days are much longer at these latitudes during the summer and much safer sailing could take place by sunlight. What these merchants could not have anticipated was solid ice. In a letter to King Henry VIII, Thorne appealed to the king's sense of rivalry. He noted that Portugal already had explored the east, and Spain had explored the west. Thorne wrote, "So that now rest to be discovered the said North parts, the which it seemeth to mee, is onely your charge and dutie. Because the situation of this your Realme is thereunto neerest and aptest of all other."

With two ships, the *Mary Guildford* and the *Samson,* Rut followed the route of the fishing fleets across the Atlantic to Newfoundland. He met storms and icebergs, and one ship was lost. Rather than strike ice, Rut turned southward toward Norumbega, as New England was then called. En route he passed several fishing ships from France and Portugal. One of these ships took a letter from Rut to King Henry VIII, the very first letter to be "mailed" from North America to Europe. In it he says, "The third day of August we entered into a good haven, called Saint John, and there we founde eleven saile of Normans, and one Brittaine, and two Portugall Barkes, and all a fishing." This is a good reminder that extensive and unrecorded voyages were made throughout these years by several competing nations, which, at least for the purposes of fishing, could overlook their national rivalries—and even carry mail.

Rut made it all the way to Florida and into the Spanish West Indies. He still planned to sail to China to meet the Great Khan. Rut tried to harbor in Santo Domingo to trade but he feared Spanish betrayal, especially after stray cannon fire, shot perhaps only as a welcome, nearly hit his ship. The warden who fired the shot claimed he was only following orders to protect the fortress. In any case, Rut decided to leave quickly. By the next season, he was back in Europe. Following Rut's voyage, which accomplished nothing, the English had no interest in North America for many decades, apart from codfishing.

There was only one curious exception. It was the fishing and pleasure cruise of Richard Hore in 1536. Some 30 gentlemen came along on this cruise just to see Newfoundland. They did not, however, expect to run out of food, but that is what happened. Several men died of starvation; some resorted to cannibalism. As Richard Hakluyt related the story:

> [S]uch was the famine that increased among them from day to day, that they were forced to seeke to relieve themselves of her-bes being to little purpose to satisfie their insatiable hunger, in the fields and deserts here and there, the fellowe killed his mate while hee stouped to take up a roote for his reliefe, and cutting out pieces of his body whome hee had murthered [murdered], broyled [broiled] the same on coles and greedily devoured them. . . . [When accosted by his fellows] he that had the broyled meate, burst out into these wordes, If thou wouldest needes knowe, the broyled meate I had, was such a piece of a mans buttocke.

As luck would have it, a French ship soon appeared, which they promptly plundered. King Henry VIII, embarrassed by the whole affair, reimbursed the French out of his own pocket.

It is no wonder that the English gave up exploring North America. Only the French continued to do so, and they would be the first to make a solid claim of the northern Atlantic coast as a French possession. By a quirk of fate, they also were given official permission to do so. In 1533, French king Francis I arranged for the marriage of his son to Florentine Catherine de' Medici. He also had her uncle, Pope Clement VII, officially alter the Treaty of 1494, which had divided the world between the Spanish and Portuguese. The French now were allowed to explore and claim regions unoccupied by Christians.

3

French, Spanish, and English Failures 1521–1590

NEARLY A DECADE AFTER GIOVANNI DA VERRAZANO'S VOYAGE, the French resumed their exploration of North America. An explorer named Jacques Cartier made three separate voyages. These would be the first expeditions to explore a good thousand miles into the North American interior. They also provided a detailed account of the region's people and geography.

JACQUES CARTIER'S FIRST VOYAGE

Little is known about Jacques Cartier except that he was born in 1491 in Saint-Malo, on the northwest coast of France. He married into a wealthy ship-owning family, and as a young man he sailed to Brazil and perhaps Newfoundland. He was probably the most skilled navigator and cartographer in France at the time.

Two ships under the command of Cartier left the port of Saint-Malo on April 20, 1534. The ships Cartier took on this voyage bore about 60 tuns manned by a crew of 61 men each. His orders from the king were primarily to discover a passage to China, but also to find a source of gold and silver. Clearly, it was international rivalry with Spain that prompted this part of the expedition. They reached Newfoundland in a remarkably swift 20 days, heading straight across the Atlantic at about 48°N. The account Cartier composed, probably later copied and altered by someone else, offers remarkable descriptions of the native wildlife. For example, at the Isle of Birds, as he called it (it is known as Funk

Jacques Cartier explored the St. Lawrence River in 1535 and claimed parts of Canada for France. There are no contemporary portraits of Cartier. The one above by Théophile Hamel (ca. 1844) imagines how he might have looked.

Island today and is located just off Newfoundland), he encountered the great auk, which is now extinct.

> *Some of these birds are as large as geese, being black and white with a beak as big as a crow's. They are always in the water, not being able to fly in the air, inasmuch as they have only small wings about the size of one's hand, with which however they move as quickly along the water as other birds fly through the air. And these birds are so fat that it is marvellous. We call them apponats and our two long-boats were laden with them as with stones, in less than half an hour. Of these, each of our ships salted four or five casks, not counting those we were able to eat fresh.*

His crew managed to capture and eat a polar bear that was swimming out to the island from the mainland. They found "his flesh was as good to eat as that of a two year old heifer [cow]." On another island, they found puffins with red beaks and feet. Later in the trip they saw a walrus, which Cartier described as a great beast. He wrote that they are "large like oxen, have two tusks in their jaw like elephant's tusks and swim about in the water."

Cartier's account also gives detailed and precise geographical descriptions and fairly accurate measurements of distance and latitude. He also had no delusions about the promise of these first islands for future exploitation—nearly everywhere all he could see were barren rocks. He admitted, "I did not see one cart-load of earth and yet I landed in many places. Except at Mont Sablon [in Labrador] there is nothing but moss and short stunted shrub."

Cartier made his way south toward Prince Edward Island. He began to find more fertile land, covered with wild peas and berries. He believed the region not only would make good farmland, but also that the cedars and spruce could be made into sturdy masts for ships. This area also was more heavily populated, and at one point his ship met a fleet of some 40 or 50 canoes. The Native Americans probably wanted to trade and followed Cartier. They displayed their furs and spoke to the French in their own language, which obviously the Frenchmen could not understand. Cartier seems to have panicked, because he fired a cannon to frighten them away. He did eventually trade with them, though, exchanging knives and iron goods for furs. Unknowingly, Cartier had stumbled on what would become one of the most important resources of the future colony.

The Native Peoples Cartier traded with were the Laurentian Iroquois, or Stadaconans, named after their city, Stadacona (present-day Quebec). By the beginning of the seventeenth century, these people had completely disappeared, either from disease, warfare, or migration. Cartier's description of their customs and diet can be considered one of the earliest ethnographic studies of a North American First Nation—as they are called in Canada. He describes shaven heads adorned with a long tuft of hair at the top tied up with leather, their custom of rubbing someone's arms and chest as a way to express thanks, as well as their methods of fishing for mackerel, growing corn, and drying figs and other fruits and beans.

Cartier also described an example of misunderstanding between these two cultures. As he had done before, Cartier set up a cross decorated with a shield bearing the fleur-de-lis from the French flag. It included the motto Vive Le Roy de France (Long Live the King of France). These crosses probably served many purposes: as a directional marker, as a way of thanking God for a safe journey, but most important, they marked territory as belonging to France. The Stadaconan's chief, Donnaconna, protested the cross. Cartier believed this meant the land belonged to the chief and that the French were not welcome. The very fact that Cartier recorded this at least shows he had some misgivings over claiming the land without the permission of the inhabitants. He gave them some shirts, red caps, and brass chains, hoping that these items would satisfy them. Two of the chief's sons boarded Cartier's ship. It seems unlikely that they understood they were being taken to France. Within a week, Cartier was heading back across the Atlantic. He arrived at Saint-Malo on September 5.

Although there exists only Cartier's account of the initial interaction of the chieftain's sons with the French, Donnaconna may have believed he was sealing an alliance with the French. He may have thought this would guarantee exclusive trading privileges or perhaps that the French would help fend off rival tribes. The two Iroquois youths, who came to be called Domagaya and Taignoaguy, dressed like Frenchmen and learned a bit of the language. Someone in France even made a written vocabulary of the Stadaconan's language.

CARTIER'S SECOND VOYAGE

With remarkable speed, Cartier's second voyage was planned and financed with a worthy patron, Philippe Chabot de Brion, an admiral of France. Cartier was given three ships: *La Grande Hermine* of more than 100 tuns, *La Petite Hermine* of about 60 tuns, and *L'Émerillon,* the smallest at about 40 tuns. Cartier and his crew left in May 1535, reaching the other side of the Atlantic in about two months. After negotiating some bays and islands, on August 10 his ships entered St. Lawrence Bay, named for the early Christian martyr Saint Lawrence. It was along this great highway of water, the sons of Donnaconna pointed out, that he would find the great Kingdom of Saguenay. They also told him that farther on they would come to "Canada."

For some reason, Cartier did not trust Domagaya and Taignoaguy. Instead of proceeding along the St. Lawrence River, he ordered his boats to continue searching the gulf for a passage. They did eventually make their way upriver toward the region called Canada, after marveling at

In this painting, Native Americans wave to Jacques Cartier and his crew as they journey up the St. Lawrence River in 1535. Until the winter of 1541–1542, Cartier and the Native Americans had friendly encounters.

the beluga whales and walruses, and met up with Donnaconna. It was there that the chief again saw his two sons after their long absence. With all parties convinced of each other's goodwill, Cartier then proceeded to Stadacona. Donnaconna, however, seems to have believed that if Cartier proceeded on to the next large settlement, Hochelaga, he might prefer to have the Hochelagans as allies instead, so Donnaconna sought to forestall Cartier. To this end, he presented Cartier with what he considered a rare and precious gift: a young girl, his own niece, and two young boys, one of which was his son. In return for this present, Cartier was asked not to visit Hochelaga. Ending his exploration here was not an option, so Cartier refused. Nonetheless, he took the children onboard and made what he believed was a reciprocal gift of swords and a wash basin. Clearly there was some serious miscommunication here.

To impress his guests, Cartier's men fired their guns. The Stadaconans were so frightened that they "began to shriek and howl in such a very loud manner that one would have thought hell had emptied itself there." What can only be described as mayhem followed. Donnaconna still wanted to keep Cartier from going on to Hochelaga. Painted black and dressed as horned devils, three men appeared as emissaries from the local god Cudouagny, who had predicted that if they went all would meet their doom in the ice and snow. Cartier and his men laughed, assured that their own god would protect them. According to Cartier's accounts, realizing that this scheme had also failed, Donnaconna suggested that Cartier leave behind some men in good faith and only then would he let his sons act as guides. Cartier—at this point thoroughly fed up with what he considered to be their treachery—decided to press on without his Native guides.

Relations with Native Americans improved greatly as the French sailed up the St. Lawrence. Cartier wrote: "These people came toward our boats in as friendly and familiar a manner as if we had been natives of the country, bringing us great store of fish and of whatever else they possessed, in order to obtain our wares, stretching forth their hands toward heaven and making many gestures and signs of joy." They were once again offered children, a girl of about eight or nine. They refused a little boy of two or three as too young.

They reached Hochelaga at the current site of Montreal. There they met with an equally happy and welcoming population. Cartier gave presents of knives, beads, and other trifles. The locals filled the French boats with fish and bread made of cornmeal. These were probably the first white men the Hochelagans had ever set their eyes upon. Historians think that they may have thought of them as superhuman. They expected Cartier to cure their paralyzed chief, along with other sick people. Cartier did not wait around long enough to have his healing powers put to the test. Most important, he had realized by this point that the rapids upriver from the settlement were not navigable.

Cartier also realized he would not be able to make the passage back to France in the winter. In a small fort on the shoreline in Stadacona, Cartier and his men braved their first Canadian winter. During this time, Cartier had ample opportunity to witness the customs of the Laurentian Iroquois in detail, and he recorded many remarkable things. He noted their almost complete lack of private property, their communal living, and their custom of men taking several wives. It was also here that Cartier took his first puffs of tobacco—which he found so hot that it reminded him of ground pepper.

Their winter stay was not a pleasant one. Not only did the snow begin to fall and their casks freeze solid, but a disease struck both Iroquois and Frenchmen alike. Their symptoms appear to have been scurvy, brought on by severe vitamin C deficiency. Gums bled, teeth fell out, and swollen and blackened limbs appeared on practically the entire crew, 25 of whom died. It was not until the Iroquois offered them a concoction of bark from the arborvitae (which means "tree of life" in Latin) that they were cured.

Meanwhile, probably to get rid of Cartier, Chief Donnaconna made up a fantastic story of the wealthy kingdom of Saguenay to the north of Stadacona. The lure of gold and jewels was enough to make Cartier believe anything. He knew that to convince the French at home that Saguenay really existed he would have to bring the chief and his sons back with him. Cartier kidnapped them and sailed back to France with a handful of children he had been given as presents.

CARTIER'S THIRD VOYAGE

Cartier arrived back in France in summer 1536. He was ready to make preparations for another voyage. Donnaconna was presented to the king, and Cartier further expounded on the riches that could be found at Saguenay, now adding spices. King Francis, who was dealing with war against Spain, was not interested. Over the next few years, Donnaconna and all but one girl among the Native Americans who had been brought to France had died, probably from smallpox and measles.

Cartier set out on his third voyage in May 1541. By this time, the French had abandoned hope of reaching China. Their goal was to build a permanent settlement from which they would conquer Saguenay. The king wanted a noble ruler for the future colony and Jean-François de La Roque, sieur de Roberval, a wealthy French nobleman, was appointed leader of the entire venture. Roberval did not leave France until a year after Cartier did. By this time, Cartier's efforts to find Saguenay had failed miserably.

Cartier's third voyage was ill-fated from the start. It did not help that the crew included many freed criminals, including women. Hiring men was too difficult because they could make more money on fishing ships. A handful of noblemen, eager to carve out little kingdoms in the new colony, also came along.

It took about three months before they made it back to Stadacona, where Cartier told the people that their chief, Donnaconna, had died in France. To calm the locals, he lied and said that the other Iroquois had married and were living happily in France. About eight miles (twelve km) from the Native settlement, he then proceeded to build his colony. It was supposed to be a base for their conquest of Saguenay. The fort was surrounded by gardens and animals brought from Europe. They also began to mine for metals. They named the settlement Charlesbourg-Royal after the son of King Francis I. Two small ships were sent to France with samples of diamonds and gold. In the end, they proved to be quartz crystals and fool's gold (pyrite, a compound of iron and sulfur).

Cartier spent about a month searching upstream of Montreal, trying to figure out how to get past the waterfalls and rapids. After having to carry the boats overland twice, he finally just gave up. Relations with the Native Americans back at the fort turned sour and the French were attacked, leading to several deaths. Scurvy hit once again and, while waiting for Roberval to arrive with reinforcements, the food began to run out. It became apparent to Cartier that if he stayed at the fort he could lose everything, including his life. In June 1542, he decided to head home with his three remaining ships containing all the surviving colonists. They also contained barrels of what he believed to be gold and jewels. Nothing could have been worse than returning home empty-handed.

On the return voyage Cartier's ships met up with Roberval's around Newfoundland. Roberval apparently had been busy the past year privateering—that is, seizing Portuguese and English ships to finance his voyage—and was well stocked and well armed. Cartier tried in vain to convince him to give up and return home, but Roberval ordered him to stay. Rather than do so and face further disaster, Cartier's ships escaped by cover of night. They left Canada and dreams of fabulous wealth behind for good.

Roberval, however, would not give up so easily. The nobles who came with him were also there for conquest and profit and hoped to

AN EXTRAORDINARY YOUNG WOMAN

One of the most fantastic—although not necessarily true—stories in the era of exploration involves a particular couple on Jean-François de La Roque, sieur de Roberval's ship. The young woman, Marguerite, a relative of Roberval's, was accompanying him with the goal of marrying a suitable husband when she arrived in New France. She fell in love, though, with one of the crew and began to carry on secretly with her new love. Their relationship was concealed by Marguerite's old handmaid, a peasant woman named Bastienne, but apparently was not concealed well enough. The general found out and decided to maroon the girl and her maid on a tiny, desolate island in the Gulf of St. Lawrence. Marguerite's love managed to escape and joined them. By winter, they were growing weak and sick and the sailor soon died. After some months, Marguerite gave birth to an infant who promptly died. Soon after, the handmaid also died. Marguerite managed to survive another two years by hunting wild animals, including polar bears, and was then miraculously picked up by French fishermen and taken home. This exemplary story of courage and fortitude was passed on to the king's sister, Marguerite de Navarre, who used it in her collection of stories titled *The Heptameron*.

receive estates once the job was complete. They even brought along their wives with the intention of raising families comfortably in their new possessions.

Roberval and the crew continued the search for Saguenay. He had no more luck than Cartier had. Near the site of Cartier's Charlesbourg-Royal, he built a large and well-defended fort on a high mountain named France-Roy. Although they planted vegetables for the winter, they did not have enough food. The group also suffered from scurvy, and about 50 died from it. By spring, the remaining men set off to find Saguenay. They, too, were stopped by rapids and powerful currents. By summer 1543, they abandoned the fort and sailed back to France.

That would be the last of France's exploration of Canada until the seventeenth century. Their claim remained on the maps, as did the imaginary Saguenay. France itself would be torn by violent wars of religion for many decades. The last thing anyone had the energy or effort to search for was fabulous wealth, let alone a passage to China. As for the Laurentian Iroquois, they disappeared entirely and, in the course of the sixteenth century, were replaced by Huron and other tribes whom the French encountered when they returned to Canada with Samuel Champlain.

SPAIN IN NORTH AMERICA

Despite the failure of the Spanish to gain a foothold in North America along its southern coast, news of an incredible fortune made by Spaniard Hernán Cortés' conquest of the Aztec Empire in Mexico spread throughout Spain. Other Spanish explorers wanted to find their own kingdoms to conquer, and Florida was one possibility. Spanish explorer Juan Ponce de León had been the first European to set foot on Florida, which he claimed for the Spanish Crown. He later attempted to found a colony there in 1521, but the settlement had to be abandoned. Lucas Vásquez de Ayllón failed miserably along the Atlantic coast later that decade. There was another attempt by Pánfilo de Narváez in 1528 to set up a colony on the gulf side of Florida near Tampa Bay. This, too, ended in disaster.

Still the Spanish continued to explore, hoping to find another great empire, particularly after Francisco Pizarro spectacularly defeated the Inca of Peru in the 1530s. The most incredible venture inspired by this was a search conducted by Francisco Vásquez de Coronado for the mythical Seven Cities of Cíbola from 1539 to 1542. He trekked across New Mexico, Texas, and Kansas. At the same time, Francisco de Ulloa explored lower California, followed by voyages by Juan Rodrí-guez Cabrillo as far north as Bodega Bay. All these were part of a care-fully timed Spanish effort between the late 1530s and early 1540s to extend its lands to the north from the Atlantic to the Pacific. What lay in between was still a mystery.

Hernando de Soto explored southeastern North America. Having made a fortune for himself in Peru, he was now anxious to find his own empire. He set out in 1539, landing in Tampa Bay on Florida's Gulf Coast, and went north. He met and fought many Native Ameri-cans on his journey through what is now Georgia, South Carolina, over the Blue Ridge Mountains, and into Alabama. His expedition went as far as Mississippi and Arkansas, his army growing weaker and shrinking every day. Finally, de Soto died of a fever along the Missis-sippi River. His journey had proved that there was no great kingdom to conquer in North America and only the vaguest hope of finding precious metals.

International rivalry became the motive for further exploration. The French had by this point mapped the Atlantic coast under Giovanni da Verrazano. Jacques Cartier already had claimed a good portion of North America. The French had proved that they were interested in coloniza-tion, even if they were not yet successful at it. Spain needed to found more colonies to prevent the French from controlling all of North America.

The viceroy of New Spain (modern-day Mexico) sent Tristán de Luna y Arellano to found settlements in the interior that could be linked by roads to the coast. Luna y Arellano began his journey in June 1559. Despite a hurricane that destroyed most of his ships, he moved north from modern-day Pensacola, Florida, to the Alabama River. Food shortages were a serious problem and the local inhabitants avoided the Spanish, probably the result of having experienced disastrous encoun-ters with de Soto years before. Luna y Arellano's men basically followed de Soto's route at this point, and met with equally disastrous results. They reached the border of present-day Tennessee before giving up.

At the same time, Spain tried to found a settlement on the Atlan-tic coast. The site of Santa Elena, in present-day South Carolina, was chosen as the best spot to spoil French efforts. Angel de Villafañe was ordered to take about 70 colonists to a point at 33°N, but they found that the site was poor. After a hurricane destroyed some of their ships, they abandoned the effort.

A SPANISH FOOTHOLD IN FLORIDA

St. Augustine in present-day Florida is the oldest continuously occupied city in what is now the United States. It was founded on August 28, 1565. The fine stone fort that remains there today, the Castillo San Marcos, was built in the late seventeenth century. From this site there were Spanish voyages of exploration up the coast. Pedro Menéndez de Avilés had the idea that the Chesapeake Bay, or Bahía de Santa María as the Spanish called it, extended 1,200 miles (1,931 km) inland. He believed it could be used to transport silver from the mines in Mexico. It might even connect with the Pacific Ocean.

Menéndez was given the right to exploit this region as its future ruler. This meant he could enslave the indigenous populations to work on plantations. He also would set up missions and would convert as many people as possible to Catholicism. At the center of his colony would be the city of Santa Elena. It was located near Port Royal Sound, South Carolina. Menéndez commanded Spanish explorer Juan Pardo to investigate the interior with the intention of finding a road to Zacatecas, a Spanish city located in northern Mexico.

Pardo's first expedition took place in 1566–1567 and included 125 soldiers. Because the explorers did not bring much food, Pardo and his men were told to take what they could from the Native populations as tribute, or contribution, by force. Pardo, thus, was forced to go from settlement to settlement traveling north through North Carolina and Tennessee. He built several forts and left men behind to deal with the Native Americans, peoples who would later come to form the Catawba, Cherokee, and Creek chiefdoms. This voyage was cut short when Pardo was ordered back to defend Santa Elena from possible French attack.

A second voyage was planned. Pardo was ordered to establish friendly relations with the Native Peoples, to tell them that they were now Spanish subjects, and to leave behind monks who could instruct them in Catholicism. Pardo and his men once again headed north through the Carolinas and Tennessee. The forts they left behind,

In 1565, Pedro Menéndez de Avilés (*kneeling, in black*) founded St. Augustine, Florida, the first permanent European settlement in the Americas. Today it is believed that St. Augustine was where the first Catholic mass was held.

however, were never well manned, so they were never able to control the Native Peoples the way Menéndez had planned. In the end, only St. Augustine and Spanish Florida remained as a legacy of Spain's efforts to control the Southeast.

THE ENGLISH IN NORTH AMERICA

During much of this time, the Spanish also were engaged in trying to put down the Protestant rebels in the Netherlands. The English tried to help the Dutch by lending money and sending troops but also by engaging in privateering that preyed on Spanish shipping. This led to the English once again becoming interested in overseas ventures. As early as the 1560s, English privateer John Hawkins began selling African slaves illegally in the Spanish West Indies, as well as seizing merchant ships. By the end of the decade, trade between England and Spain was officially suspended, and engagements at sea became violent. It was in the wake of this that Sir Francis Drake began a spectacular run of raiding voyages against Spanish colonies, one of which, starting in 1577, succeeded in circumnavigating the globe.

In 1576, Humphrey Gilbert's book *Discourse of a Discoverie for a New Passage to Cataia* was published. The book's purpose was to earn support for a voyage through the Northwest Passage across the Sierra Nevada Mountains, out the Strait of Anian, and all the way to China. Such a voyage, though, was purely fictional. The first voyages to attempt to find a "northwest passage" were led by English explorer Martin Frobisher. Having been to West Africa and having successfully led privateering voyages against the Spanish, he was a logical choice for the job. Frobisher met with misfortune from the very start. There were bad storms and a collision early in the trip. A passage, now called Frobisher's Strait, was eventually found extending 150 miles (241 km) inland. To impress investors, Frobisher gathered up pyrite, a type of iron ore they believed was real gold. The excitement sparked off what might be considered the first gold rush.

With numerous wealthy investors, including Queen Elizabeth herself, a joint-stock company was formed. By 1577, Frobisher was ready to make a second voyage. The expedition mined 200 tons of pyrite. It was once again fool's gold, and once again no one back in England successfully tested it. By the time the third voyage was arranged in 1578, there were even more investors. The greed for gold appears to have entirely replaced the desire to find the passage to China and the promise of trade with Asia. This time they mined 1,350 tons of pyrite. It was finally revealed to be fool's gold. The entire enterprise ended in utter failure and bankruptcy.

There were further attempts to find the Northwest Passage. Most notably, three voyages were led by English explorer John Davis from 1585 to 1587. But attention shifted south to what would become Virginia, named for Elizabeth I, who was known as the Virgin Queen. The interest in this region first came to the queen's attention through one of her court favorites, Sir Walter Raleigh. Raleigh was issued official patents to found and rule over the colony. He chose two men to lead an expedition to choose a suitable site, Philip Amadas and Arthur Barlowe. They left in two small ships in 1584, crossing to the West Indies before making their way north to the Carolina coast. They claimed it for

England, then met the native Algonquian-speaking peoples in a place later called Roanoke Island.

As with other first encounters, the two peoples were on friendly terms and exchanged gifts. Given the mild climate and the arable land, the English naturally favored this site for their future colony. The generous Native Americans shared their corn, pumpkins, fish, and game with them. The Englishmen thought they had found the site for their future colony. They had little reason to look much farther. They quickly returned home with two Native Americans and glowing reports of the bounty of this land: "The soile is the most plentifull, sweete, fruitfull, and wholesome of all the world."

By 1585, the English were ready to set up the new colony. Sir Richard Grenville was put in charge of the voyage. Some 600 people in all went. The governor of the new colony was to be Ralph Lane. Scientist Thomas Hariot came along to study the plants, animals, and Native Peoples. John White came to illustrate their discoveries, which were later copied and printed by Theodor de Bry. These depictions became one of the principal ways Europeans learned about the Native American culture of this region and period.

The ships made their way across the Atlantic in April 1585. There, they investigated Puerto Rico, built a fort and a small boat to replace one that had sunk off Portugal, and picked up fresh supplies. Finally, along the Carolina coast, they arrived at two Native American villages, Pomeiooc and Secotan. Relations soon soured when a silver cup was stolen, and Grenville decided to burn a village as punishment. Eventually, the colonists were set ashore at Roanoke, with Ralph Lane as governor. Grenville himself returned to England.

Roanoke was not a particularly good site for a colony. The waters were shallow, so large ships carrying supplies could not reach the site. The English would have to depend on the Native Americans for supplies. In addition, Governor Lane was a poor diplomat. Fearing an attack, he decided to attack first. His men killed Wingina, the local chieftain. What may have happened next can only be guesswork. The colony may have been destroyed then and there had not a relief mission under Sir Francis Drake accidentally arrived in 1586, fresh from successful raids in the West Indies and a sack of St. Augustine. The colonists begged Drake to take them home. Soon thereafter, Grenville returned and found the colony completely abandoned. He left 18 men behind to maintain the fort. By the time the next ship arrived, they had all disappeared.

Raleigh simply would not give up his plan for a colony in Virginia. In Raleigh's second attempt, John White, a person who was considered more sensitive to relations with the Native Americans, was to be governor. This time whole families were sent. There was even a baby born, White's grandchild, appropriately named Virginia. They intended this colony to be permanent. Although the original plans were to settle along the Chesapeake Bay, which had deeper harbors and still good relations with the Native Americans there, the ships landed once again at Roanoke and decided to stay there. This would prove to be a fatal mistake. All efforts to make peace failed. Even worse, no relief voyages could be arranged back in England, because every boat was needed to fend off the Spanish Armada, which had been sent to invade England in 1588.

By the time the English were able to return to Virginia in 1590, the colony had been destroyed. All they found was the word CROATOAN carved in a tree. What happened to the colonists is a mystery. The English settlers might have been killed. They might have left this word as a clue that they had melded with a group of Native Peoples. There remains a tradition that this was indeed the colonists' fate. Apparently English surnames and even English words were later found among the Native tribes.

4

Europeans Colonize and Contest Northeastern America
Early Seventeenth Century

AT THE BEGINNING OF THE SEVENTEENTH CENTURY, EUROPEANS looked back on nearly a century of almost total failure in North America. It is true that, in terms of exploration alone, much of the coastline had been accurately charted, as had some of the interior. But there was no fabulously wealthy empire to conquer like the Aztec or Inca. There was no gold or spices. No northwest passage had been discovered, nor would one be for another few centuries. And most important, no permanent settlement, apart from tiny St. Augustine, was founded in the modern-day United States until the seventeenth century.

The colonization of North America was accomplished through dogged determination, as well as a refocusing of motives from plunder to settlement, agriculture, and trade in beaver skins to supply the growing demand for fur felt hats. Perhaps most important, and sadly, the colonization was accomplished through the slow disappearance of the Native Peoples due to disease. The full impact of European diseases such as smallpox and measles was not felt for many years, but these diseases made the colonial experience of North America very different than anywhere in the world. Settlers would, once they managed to feed themselves, have a much easier time maintaining their colonies and populating them. But at first their efforts were not so smoothly realized.

JAMESTOWN

The Jamestown colony was the first permanent English settlement in North America. Founded in 1607, its first 105 settlers were led by Christopher Newport. The site they chose was 60 miles (96 km) from the mouth of the Chesapeake Bay along the James River. When the colonists arrived, the Algonquian peoples lived there, allied in a large confederacy led by Powhatan—their *werowance,* or big chief. For some reason many of the settlers did not intend to work hard and depended on the Algonquian for food. The Algonquian cooperated, expecting to profit from English trade. They also hoped the English would help fight their enemies. Despite this help, the colony barely survived. There were only 38 men left when a relief ship arrived in 1608.

The colony was paid for by the Virginia Company. Its investors decided that stern measures were required and placed Captain John Smith in charge. He was an experienced but harsh commander. He forced the colonists to build houses and plant food while he maintained strict discipline. But even he took food from the Algonquian. In return, the Algonquian decided to starve them out. At this they nearly succeeded. In the winter of 1609–1610, the majority of settlers starved to death. Some resorted to cannibalism.

The investors back in England were determined to occupy the entire region with force. Within the next few years they did just that. They sent out additional colonists, supplies, and weapons. The Algonquian leader, Powhatan, sent his daughter Pocahontas to come to friendly terms with the English. There is a famous episode in which Pocahontas saved John Smith's life by declaring her love for him moments before he was to be executed. If it actually happened at all, it was probably a staged reconciliation between the English and the Algonquian. Modern scholars now believe that Smith invented the story to enhance his own reputation.Pocahontas married tobacco farmer John Rolfe and went to England, where she became a celebrity. She died before getting a chance to return to the Americas.

The long-term success of this colony was due primarily to their discovery of a cash crop with which they could make the venture profitable and self-sustaining. Pocahontas's husband had planted tobacco, which would ultimately seal the economic fate of this region for centuries. To

John Smith was chosen to be one of the leaders of the Jamestown colony in Virginia in 1607. Smith was taken captive by Chief Powhatan and, as the story goes, was saved by the chief's daughter, Pocahontas (*depicted above*). Historians believe Smith made up the story to enhance his own reputation.

set up large tobacco plantations, the colonists moved the Native Americans out as English families were brought in. Eventually the two groups engaged in open warfare. In the end, the company went broke, and the Crown was forced to take control. After a few decades, the Native Peoples succumbed in alarming numbers to European diseases. In the coming years, African slaves were brought in to work in the plantations. The first such slave actually arrived as early as 1619.

There also were further attempts by the English to explore and settle the northern coastline of the newly renamed New England. Captain John Smith made a voyage in the summer of 1614 and mapped the region between Cape Cod, Massachusetts, and the Penobscot Bay, Maine's largest coastal waterway. His glowing account about the prospects of the region, "Description of New England," was published in England in 1616 and was meant to attract investors. He also considered whaling in this area, but "We found this whale-fishing a costly conclusion. We saw many and spent much time in chasing them, but could not kill any." Little could Smith have guessed how important whaling would become to New England in later centuries. Instead of whale hunting, they fell back on fishing and fur trading, but neither was enough to impress investors at home, even though Smith reminded them of how the Dutch had grown so fantastically wealthy on such a lowly business as fishing. In the next few years, Smith made further attempts to settle New England, all of which met with failure. His dream of populating the region with small land-holding freemen, rather than aristocratic estates, would come to pass when the Pilgrims arrived seeking religious freedom in 1620.

THE FRENCH AND CHAMPLAIN

France, too, became interested again in North America around the turn of the seventeenth century. François Gravé led a voyage of exploration up the St. Lawrence in 1603. Gravé was joined by Samuel de Champlain. It was Champlain's observations and report of further waterways in the interior, which he learned about from the Algonquian and Montagnais tribes, that kept alive the idea of trade and colonization in this region. By this time, the Laurentian Iroquois whom Cartier had met earlier in the century had completely disappeared.

The next major French efforts at colonization were led by Pierre de Gua, sieur de Monts, who was granted a monopoly on exploitation of the region and its fur trade in 1603. As lieutenant general, it was also his job to populate the colony, and in 1604 he left France with 120 settlers. Champlain was also on this voyage. He was given the task of finding a suitable site after their original location along the St. Croix River was found to be too harsh. Champlain explored the coast beyond Cape Cod in several successive voyages over the course of three years. In the end they chose a site, Port Royal, on Nova Scotia facing the Bay of Fundy. The settlement was then turned over to another nobleman, Jean de Biencourt, the sieur de Poutrincourt, after sieur de Monts's patent was revoked in 1607.

The fur trade was the engine that was driving exploration in many parts of the northeastern region of North America. It was the fur trade that drew Samuel de Champlain to found a permanent trading post

BEAVER HATS

Although a beaver's fur was useful as warm protective covering, many Europeans wanted it more because of its soft underfur, which could be made into felt for hats. Beaver hats became fashionable at the end of the sixteenth century and stayed fashionable in a variety of styles for more than 200 years. In the seventeenth and eighteenth centuries, the fashion was for a three-cornered, or tricorner, hat, and it might be trimmed with a ribbon, an insignia, or a feather. The best beaver furs that traders could buy were those that already had been worn by Native Americans as clothes or blankets. That was because regular use had taken off some of the outer fur and helped prepare the animal skin for feltmaking. Hatmakers cut the fur from the pelt, smoothed the hair, and used heat and pressure to make it into felt. Beaver felt held its shape better and lasted longer than any other material that was used in hatmaking, and hatmaking was a big business. Until quite recent times, few European men ever would have gone out in public without a hat. In fact, a beaver hat, which would have been expensive, held its shape so well over time that it could be handed down for generations.

at Quebec in 1608 and to explore to the north and west. He already knew the St. Lawrence River Valley well, through trading at Tadoussac, exploring the river as far as Montreal Island, and traveling up the Saguenay and Richelieu rivers. His goals at Quebec were to establish a permanent settlement, trade furs, explore the region, introduce Christianity to the people, and still try to find a river route to the Pacific.

Before he could do any of these things, however, he had to secure his new community, as well as trading and diplomatic relationships with the local Native Peoples. These were the Huron, Algonquian, and Montagnais. These communities traded with the French and, in return, the French helped defend them from their enemies. In 1609, the Huron were attacked by their old enemies, the Iroquois Confederacy, who occupied territory south of Lake Ontario. The Huron expected and received Champlain's help. Although few in number, the French had gunpowder weapons and they helped the Huron drive off their enemies.

The French and Huron victory at a battle near the southern tip of Lake Champlain in July 1609 had a huge impact. The French did indeed cement their relationship with the Huron. They also made enemies of the Iroquois, whom they would fight for much of the next century. This gave the Iroquois a good reason to welcome the Dutch traders when they came. The Five Nations of the Iroquois Confederacy (a confederation of five Native American tribes—the Mohawk, the Oneida, the Onondaga, the Cayuga, and the Seneca) found the Dutch willing to trade weapons and other metal tools for furs.

Champlain understood that success in the fur trade lay in finding routes and making friends. Until his death in 1635, he either traveled or sponsored the journeys of others to explore and map the region. He needed money to do this, so he regularly published accounts of his journeys to promote the colony.

Champlain and his men explored much of the region. By 1635, they had reached as far west as what is now Green Bay, Wisconsin. They also had gone as far south as the Susquehanna River. This river has its source in what is today central New York. They had perhaps followed it down to its mouth at Chesapeake Bay.

In May 1613, after securing the safety of the settlement of Quebec, Champlain's own next major journey of exploration took him up the Ottawa River, a major tributary of the St. Lawrence River. Champlain

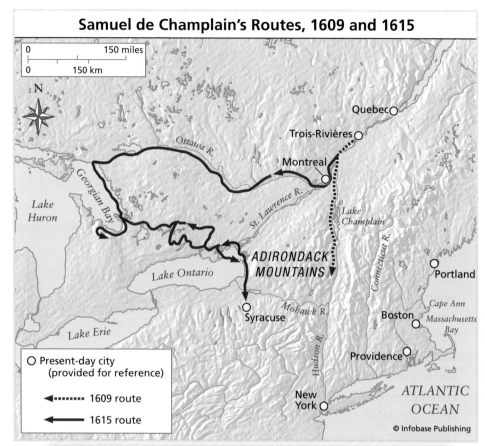

Samuel de Champlain's Routes, 1609 and 1615

In 1608, Samuel de Champlain established a French colony at Quebec. In order to attain his goals, Champlain needed to secure a friendly relationship with the Huron, Algonquian, and Montagnais Indians. His ability to establish diplomatic relations and the help he gave the Huron in driving off their enemies, the Iroquois, cemented long-time French and Huron ties.

and his crew traveled as far north as what is now Allumette Island (opposite Pembroke, Ontario) on the Ottawa River. Even though this great journey is always associated with him, Champlain was not the first European to travel this route. A young Frenchman, Nicolas de Vignau, had already been there.

Earlier, as part of a diplomatic exchange with the Algonquian, Champlain had sent Vignau to live with the tribe. In return, he had taken an Algonquian young man back to France. During his time among the Algonquian, Vignau learned the language. On his return, Vignau told

Champlain that he had paddled up the Ottawa to its source at a lake. This lake, he said, had a river to the "North Sea" (Hudson Bay). Champlain was later sure that Vignau had lied about that, but for the moment he was eager to see this sea for himself.

Champlain was traveling lightly. He had only two canoes, one Native guide, and four Frenchmen, one of whom was Vignau. They had to portage their canoes and all their supplies over land around the La Chine rapids near Montreal. These rapids had blocked Jacques Cartier's path when his expedition had sailed down the St. Lawrence in 1536. He had named them the "China rapids" because he believed that the river was the route to Asia.

Even traveling lightly, Champlain found the portage difficult. He noted that it was "no small matter for persons not accustomed to it." It was only the first of many portages. At another point, the water moved against them with "great velocity." They could not portage, and the forest was too thick. So the party had to "get into the water and drag our canoes along the shore with a rope." Champlain almost lost his hand doing this. He had a tow rope wound around his wrist to pull his canoe when it was swept into particularly fierce waters. Luckily the canoe became jammed between two rocks and he was able to "undo quickly enough rope which was wound around my hand, and which hurt me severely and came near cutting it off."

The next day, they met a party of Algonquian going in the opposite direction. The two groups visited for a while. The Algonquian told Champlain that the way ahead was harder than anything they had yet seen. Champlain exchanged one of his own party for an Algonquian guide. The new group now passed where the Gatineau River flows into the Ottawa. This is where the modern city of Ottawa is located. Their Native guide's advice saved days of difficult portages. They had been fighting the current of the south-flowing Ottawa River. Their guide directed them to make a portage to what is now Coldingham Lake, leading them to a north-flowing river. The party now was able to travel north through a series of lakes and waterways. The return journey would be down the rapids of the south-flowing Ottawa River.

They eventually reached Allumette Island. Champlain met Tessoüat, an Algonquian leader, whom he had met years before at a trading post. Tessoüat also had met Vignau before. Tessoüat denied that his people had guided Vignau to the "North Sea," and Champlain realized that Vignau had lied to him. Tessoüat told Champlain that he could get no farther that season, so Champlain began his return journey. Historians are undecided today about whether Vignau actually had seen Hudson Bay. They think that Tessoüat might have encouraged Champlain to turn back in order to maintain his own power in the region.

On Champlain's return journey, 40 canoes accompanied him as part of a celebratory farewell from the Native Americans. Champlain's group ran the rapids without any accidents and had successfully mapped parts of the region, having taken measurements of the latitude using an astrolabe. He had cemented diplomatic and trading relationships with Native American friends. He had a better idea of how the rivers might be used to head west. All this, and the whole journey had taken only three weeks. Champlain returned to France with the news.

In 1615, Champlain returned to New France for another journey of exploration. This time he was accompanied by four Récollet priests to be missionaries to the Native Americans and the small French community. The Récollets were the French branch of the Franciscan order of Catholic priests. The Récollets were not trained for such rigorous work, and in the next decade the Jesuits would replace them. In the meantime, however, they set about their tasks, and one, Father Joseph Le Caron, set off to convert the Huron.

Champlain brought new money from investors. He set off, hoping to reach Huronia, the territory of the western Huron and Lake Huron itself. Champlain's party quickly reached Allumette Island, the farthest point of his trip two years earlier. They now went farther up the Ottawa and then up the Mattawa River. They reached Lake Nipissing by late July 1615. From there, they followed the French River to Lake Huron. Champlain and his party explored the eastern shore of Georgian Bay of Lake Huron. They enjoyed the sight of what he called *La Mer Douce*, "the sweet sea." He marveled at the fertile land around the lake and the huge trout that swam in it. So fertile was the land that thousands of Huron peoples lived in the region in many villages and towns. Champlain, however, was in for a surprise. A couple of miles inland on the Midland Peninsula (near Penetanguishene, Ontario), at a Huron village called Carhagoua, there was Father Le Caron, already established. Le Caron was very surprised to see Champlain, and he celebrated mass to mark the occasion.

By the middle of the 1630s, the French had found a route to Lake Michigan. They had good trading relationships with their Native allies; however, their settlement at Quebec stayed small.

HENRY HUDSON, THE DUTCH, AND THE SWEDISH

A new European power also began its own exploration of North America—the Dutch. It was not, however, the Dutch government that supported the expeditions, nor did they even have a king or royal court that could sponsor such voyages. Rather, the expeditions were backed by the Dutch East India Company, whose main efforts lay in Asia. Part of its plans for heading to North America included searching for a northwest passage. The company hired Englishman Henry Hudson to organize a trip in 1609. Hudson already had made trips under the employ of the English Muscovy Company to find a northeast passage (above Russia). He also thought there was a passage somewhere above Virginia. The explorations of John Smith, whom he knew, seemed to confirm this idea. This, Hudson's third voyage in his ship the *Halve Maen*, was intended to sail above and across Russia to reach Asia. However, his crew would not press into the frozen Arctic. Instead, they headed west. Hudson and his crew arrived at Newfoundland, then sailed south, arriving at what is now New York Harbor on September 11, 1609. From there he sailed up a grand river as far as Albany. The river was later named after him.

According to the account left by Hudson's first mate, Robert Juet, the Native Americans they met here (Mahicans of the larger Lenni Lenape group) were eager to trade tobacco and corn for knives and other European wares. The Dutchmen did not trust them and took what the Native Americans would not willingly offer.

Although Hudson considered this venture a failure, and though he was marooned in the Arctic by a mutinous crew on his fourth voyage, the Dutch remained interested in this as-of-yet unclaimed region of the mid-Atlantic coast. In the coming years, the Dutch realized that the Iroquois had an extensive fur-trading network and hoped to profit from it. In 1614, another Dutch explorer, Adriaen Block, mapped the region. He discovered that Long Island was separate from the mainland. Block also named Manhattan and explored the Connecticut River.

Soon a new Dutch company was formed, the New Netherland Company. It set up two trading forts at New Amsterdam (present-day Manhattan) and Fort Nassau, later renamed Fort Orange (near the site of present-day Albany). Although they later were replaced by the Dutch West India Company, the Dutch traders became wealthy from their trade with the Iroquois. They competed with French trade among the Huron. This competition would have long-term historical significance.

New Amsterdam did survive as a colony and, in fact, was the first multiethnic settlement. It included Europeans of many nations, Africans, and Jews. The colony practiced religious tolerance. The Dutch street plan of Lower Manhattan can still be seen today. Many Dutch place-names survive, including the Bowery, Harlem, the Bronx, Brooklyn, and Yonkers. Later, New Amsterdam was given to the English after a war in the late-seventeenth century. In return, the English gave the Dutch the East Indian Spice Islands.

There was one other European power that helped open up this region. Starting in 1638, the Swedes set up posts along the Delaware Valley from which to trade fur. They were successful for nearly two decades, having set up forts like Fort Christina in present-day New Castle, Delaware, and small settlements throughout southern New Jersey. For a brief time the Atlantic coast was carved up by Spanish, French, English, Dutch, and Swedish colonies. It was only in 1655 that the Dutch, led by Peter Stuyvesant, marched down and seized New Sweden. The Swedish lands became part of the New Netherlands colony.

In the first decades of the seventeenth century, five major European powers had footholds on the North American continent. In the coming years, their exploration of the interior would lead to conflicts among themselves. It also led to conflicts with Native American tribes. Despite the conflicts, all Europeans would continue to rely on the Native Americans. They took advantage of Native American knowledge of the continent, even as they forced them from their lands.

5

Furs, Friars, and French Exploration

1635–1673

IN LATE SUMMER 1673, FATHER JACQUES MARQUETTE, A JESUIT priest, and Louis Jolliet, a French Canadian fur trader, had to make a big decision. They had spent the summer traveling where no European had gone before. They had led a party of men from the northern shores of Lake Michigan down to Green Bay, along the Fox River, and then by rivers and streams and occasionally on land to the Wisconsin River. Then they had gone down the river as it flowed into the Mississippi. They had followed the great Mississippi River down to where the Arkansas River flows into it, where the modern states of Arkansas and Louisiana now meet.

Marquette and Jolliet were not sure what their next move should be. Marquette wrote that he and Jolliet tried to decide "whether we should push on or remain content with the discovery which we had made." Jolliet had made an extensive map of their travels, and they had closely observed the environment, the peoples, and the vegetation. Although they had some hair-raising moments, their encounters with Native Americans along the route were generally friendly. They guessed (correctly) that they were probably no more than a two- or three-day journey from the place where the Mississippi flowed into the sea, although they were not sure if that was going to be the Atlantic Ocean or the Gulf of Mexico.

Even though they were so close to finding out, they decided to turn back. They were afraid of falling into the hands of the Spanish, and that the Native Americans ahead might be unfriendly. Most of all they hated to risk "losing the results of this voyage." Others would later get credit

Father Jacques Marquette and Louis Jolliet explored much of the Mississippi River in 1673. They traveled to within 435 miles (700 km) of the Gulf of Mexico, but they turned back to avoid running into the Spanish and hostile Native Americans.

for being the first Europeans to travel down the Mississippi to where it flowed into the Gulf of Mexico.

Marquette and Jolliet's journey reflects a lot of the practical realities of French exploration in the seventeenth century. The journey combined the desire to expand French control on the continent, to develop new sources of furs from more distant peoples, and to convert Native Americans to Christianity. Success required courage, planning, and hard work. Since the Europeans also were greatly outnumbered, it also required diplomatic skills to avoid violent confrontations and misunderstandings.

EARLY FRENCH EXPLORATIONS

In the years between the death of Samuel de Champlain in 1635 and Marquette and Jolliet's journey in 1673, French fur trappers, adventurers, Jesuit priests, and governors of the colony had expanded French interests in North America from the St. Lawrence River Valley to Lake Superior. A network of rivers and lakes made their travels deep into the continent easier. Even when rivers did not conveniently lead into one another, local Native Americans were often able to lead and assist them to good portages where they might find the shortest or most easily traveled point between two waterways. By these means, the French had made contact with a wide range of peoples. They had met and traded with the Anishinabe around Lake Superior; the Cree to the north of that lake; the Illinois, on the river that now bears their name; and the Mascoutens on the Fox River. Pierre Radisson, a French explorer and fur trader, noted they had even met "ambassadors from the nations of Nadoneseronons," probably the Dakota people, who wore buffalo skins. And Jesuit priest Jean de Quen wrote in his annual report of a great lake "as large as the Caspian Sea" called "Ouinipeg."

Much of the information about these discoveries was in colonial and Jesuit reports. However, the system of forts and missions also provided places where travelers could exchange information. For example, in 1665, Jesuit priest Claude Allouez founded a mission at Chequamegon Bay on Lake Superior, near present-day Ashland, Wisconsin, and explored around the lakeshore. In 1668, Jacques Marquette, who had recently arrived in New France, also came out to Chequamegon Bay. Later, Allouez moved to a mission at Green Bay, in the northern part of Lake Michigan. At the same time, young fur trader Louis Jolliet was also in the neighborhood, traveling with his brother Adrien. Adrien then went to join another Jesuit, Jean Peré, who was searching for copper mines on the shores of Lake Superior. It was in this area that Louis Jolliet met Marquette for the first time.

The influence of the French extended broadly into the interior of the continent, but at the same time the European population of New France stayed very small, only 3,000 in 1663. So, while the Spanish Empire used its military power to subjugate Native American peoples, and the more numerous English settlers regularly fought Native Americans over land use, the outnumbered French used commercial, diplomatic, and social relationships to secure their interests in North America.

Some of the Jesuits' adventures show how much the French relied on Native American goodwill. Claude Dablon and Gabriel Druillettes set off in May 1661 to try to establish a mission to the Cree Indians who occupied territory to the south of Hudson Bay. They planned to go up the Saguenay River from Tadoussac, the settlement at the confluence of the Saguenay and St. Lawrence rivers, into the hills and then find a river that flowed down the other side into Hudson Bay. Huron Indians were to be their guides on the first part of their journey to Lake Nekouba (Nikaubau), which was a trading center for many Native Peoples. The priests relied on Native American diplomacy to smooth their path. The previous year, Huron guides had gone ahead to arrange meetings there with other Native American nations.

The report of their difficult journey to Lake Nekouba, probably written by Dablon, appeared in the *Jesuit Relations.* He reported that they had relied heavily on Native labor and that, day after day, the party had to carry everything, as many as 40 canoes and all their baggage, around waterfalls and rapids. One day they had to "shoulder our baggage four times and twice on the day after." It took them a month to reach the lake and required 64 portages. Exhausted, they turned back.

Still they had gained useful knowledge and connections for the next explorers. Dablon noted that they had met "people from eight or ten nations, some of whom had never beheld a Frenchman" and built a body of knowledge about the region. A decade later, in 1672, another expedition, led by Jesuit Charles Albanel, successfully crossed the hills and found a route along what is now known as Rupert River, which flowed into James Bay at the southern tip of Hudson Bay.

The journey of Father Jean de Quen was also dependent on Native American labor and goodwill. After spending several years with the Montagnais in Tadoussac, Father de Quen went with them in 1647 to travel to the Porcupine nation, who lived on Lake Piékouagami (now Lake Saint-Jean). Led and aided by Montagnais guides, the party traveled up the Saguenay River and then followed a variety of lakes and waterways. The journey, de Quen wrote, involved "constant rowing against the current" and many portages. But Lake Piékouagami, when they got there, was large, "deep and full of fish . . . [and]

surrounded by flat land," but with "high mountains" in the distance. Cooperation and diplomacy were essential to successful exploration.

THE ENGLISH EXPERIENCE

While the French presence in New France stayed small, English men and women were arriving in large numbers on the Atlantic coast. By 1660, more than 70,000 were there. More than half this population was concentrated in New England and around the Chesapeake Bay, where there were also about 3,000 African slaves. Settlement was still largely clustered along the coast and easily navigable waterways, but the desire for good farmland was steadily drawing colonists into the backcountry. As they settled new communities, ordinary farmers and their families became explorers as they surveyed their towns in order for property lines to be drawn accurately.

In New England, other groups of English people were exploring. One group was comprised of men who were interested in harvesting the beautiful, tall white pine trees that made good masts for sailing ships. These lumbermen explored and mapped the area that is now New Hampshire and Maine to search for the best trees. Along the rivers near the forests, they built lumber mills to process the felled trees, and they charted rivers and settled towns such as Kittery, Wells, and Portland in Maine.

Another group of English people became explorers unintentionally. These were the people who were banished from the Massachusetts and Plymouth colonies for religious reasons. Puritan leaders who had settled there were not tolerant of anyone who disagreed with their way of doing things. In 1635, they banished one young minister, Roger Williams, who challenged their authority. Williams spent the winter sheltering with the Narragansett Indians and then, with a few followers, settled a town they called Providence in what became a few years later the separate colony of Rhode Island. Thomas Hooker, another defiant minister, took his whole congregation through the backcountry to establish a town on the Connecticut River they called Hartford.

In these ways, the English settlements expanded slowly but steadily inland. In the 1670s, these new farming communities again brought the English into conflict with the Native Americans. In New England, in the summer of 1675, a loose coalition of Native Peoples led by Metacom of the Wampanoag, whom the English called King Philip, led an

Roger Williams, a young minister, believed in religious tolerance, fair dealings with the Native Americans, and separation of church and state. For his beliefs, Williams was banished from the Plymouth colony, and he spent the winter of 1635 living with the Narragansett tribe (*depicted above*).

uprising against the English. Metacom attacked and destroyed many outlying villages. Even though what became known as King Philip's War ultimately failed, it did temporarily drive back English settlement. It would be the next century before settlers inched their way back into the territory that they had occupied before the war.

Still, conflicts over land did not bring trade with Native Americans to a halt. Through it, Englishmen continued to extend their knowledge of the West. The first known European to journey west of the Blue Ridge Mountains of Virginia was actually a German immigrant, John Lederer. He made two journeys, traveling with Native American guides and an Englishman. In 1670, he journeyed from the falls of the Rappahannock River (now Fredericksburg, Virginia) to the top of the mountains. The following year, Virginian Abraham Wood, who himself knew western Virginia well through his trade with Native Americans, recruited Thomas Batts, Robert Fallam, and a Native American guide named Perecute, of the local Appomattox people, to lead a party west. The journal of the expedition, probably written by either Batts or Fallam, noted that the party's mission was "for the finding out the ebbing and flowing Water on the other side of the Mountains." The journal is vague, but they appear to have followed the North Fork of the Roanoke River and reached as far as present-day Union, West Virginia. The trip, the journal recorded, "cost us hard labour," and finally, fearing bad weather and running short of food, the party turned back.

In 1674, Wood sponsored another journey west, though in this case the young explorers he recruited saw more of the land beyond the mountains than they had intended. Wood wrote that he sent out "two Englishmen and eight Indians" with three months of supplies to travel through the Piedmont and mountains of North Carolina to trade with the Cherokee. Unfortunately, one of the Englishmen, James Needham, was killed. The other, Gabriel Arthur, was taken prisoner by Ohio Indians. On his way home, Arthur became the first European to see what would become known as the Cumberland Gap in Tennessee and related his travels to Wood. Wood also found that those in power gave "no encouragement at all" for these kinds of enterprises, but he hoped for better days.

Alas, these days did not come quickly. Open conflict with Native Americans over land now slowed westward exploration and settlement in Virginia. As poorer farmers pursued cheaper property inland, their settlements created tensions with local Native Americans and that interfered with the trade controlled by the governor and his friends along the eastern coast. This conflict had two dimensions: One was between colonists and Native Americans concerning competition for land. The other found wealthy planters and those who traded with Native Americans on one side and poorer farmers and some wealthy men who had been shut out of Native American trade on the other. Nathaniel Bacon, one settler who had been shut out from Native American trade, encouraged poor men and settlers in the backcountry to join him in a rebellion against the governor. What began in 1675 as a war between the Susquehannock Indians, who lived north of the Potomac River, and the settlers became a larger conflict known as Bacon's Rebellion. The governor was able to crush it, but the episode slowed westward exploration and settlement.

Despite these tensions between Native Peoples and settlers in Virginia and New England, England was creating and exploring other colonies on the East Coast. In 1663 the British king, Charles II, gave a colonial charter for the Carolinas to a group of colonial proprietors who wanted to know where the best place might be to establish a town. They commissioned English sea captain Robert Sandford to explore and report on the coast. He did so, including a detailed account of the Savannah River. The owners also sent with him Henry Woodward, who was left in the Carolinas to establish relations with local Cusabo Indians, to learn their language, and to gain knowledge of the region. After the founding of Charles Town, Woodward expanded trade with the Native Americans, this time with the Westo people.

THE DUTCH PRESENCE

Meanwhile, on the Hudson River, Dutch fur traders were successful by staying relatively close to their trading posts and doing little inland exploring. The powerful Iroquois Confederacy did not want the Dutch trading directly with other tribes located farther inland and preferred to be the middlemen. The town of Beverwyck (formerly Fort Orange), which became Albany, had a significant number of fur traders among its small population, but many of these men were also farmers. One Dutch colonist, Adriaen Van Der Donck, wrote the *Account of the New Netherlands* that showed that the Dutch organized their trade very differently from the French. He wrote that few Dutchmen had been "more than seventy or eighty miles [112 or 128 km] from the river." Rather, it was the Native Americans who came "more than ten and twenty days journey" to trade with the Dutch.

Ironically, it is a French Jesuit explorer who has left one of the best surviving descriptions of this Dutch colony. Father Isaac Jogues traveled extensively around the upper Great Lakes with Father Charles Raymbaud in 1641. The following year, Jogues returned to the east and to Iroquois territory. He was captured and tortured before managing to escape to the Dutch at Albany. Jogues was impressed by the kindness the Dutch showed him even though they could not easily communicate and they had religious differences (they were Protestant and he was Catholic).

The politics of the region were transformed when, in 1664, the Dutch colony fell into English hands and was renamed New York. This change meant that the fur trading rivalry between present-day Albany and Quebec became part of a larger imperial contest between France and England that kept the two countries at war with each other for much of the next 100 years. The Five Nations of the Iroquois Confederacy tried to maneuver this situation to their advantage and formed an alliance with the English that became known as the Covenant Chain. This was a metaphor for the friendship between the two. The English supported and encouraged the Iroquois to dominate other tribes in the Northeast. This made the Iroquois more powerful, but it also kept the English colonists safe from attack and allowed economic growth. The English thus confined themselves, for the moment, behind the natural barrier of the Appalachian Mountains and the military power of the Iroquois.

HUDSON BAY AND THE FUR TRADE

While the English were slowly securing and settling colonies on the coast to the south and east of the French, they also managed to secure a claim to a vast expanse of territory to the north. This claim was around Hudson Bay, the sea route to which lay above 60°N and was open to shipping for only two months of the year. London merchants provided the money to establish trading posts, but the men who first explored the region and understood its potential as a trading center were two Frenchmen. Their actions transformed the struggle to control the continent.

The two men who led this journey of exploration from 1658 to 1660 were two French-born fur traders, Pierre-Esprit Radisson and his brother-in-law, Médard Chouart, sieur des Groseilliers. Individually, the two men already had extensive experience in the interior of the country prior to their journey. Groseilliers, born in 1618, had traveled extensively around the Great Lakes, both as a lay worker with the Jesuits and as a fur trader. It was while on a journey to Green Bay that he heard stories from local Native Americans about the rich fur territory that lay north of Lake Superior.

For his next journey, he chose as his traveling partner Radisson, who was probably around 21 in 1659. They set out with Frenchmen and Huron Indians and made their way to Green Bay. At first they were in

FATHER JEAN DE BRÉBEUF LEARNS NEW LANGUAGES

Both Native Americans and Europeans had to learn new languages as they encountered each other. Unfortunately, for the first centuries of contact there are accounts only from Europeans of how they coped with this. Each community had individuals with a skill for languages who came to act as translators. The French priest Jean de Brébeuf had a particular aptitude for languages; he spoke Huron fluently and was able to communicate in several other Native American languages. The Jesuits, formally called the Society of Jesus, to which Brébeuf belonged, were a religious order founded by Ignatius of Loyola in 1534. The Jesuits were trained in Latin and Greek, and that made them observant about the structure of language when they encountered new ones. When he arrived in Quebec in 1625, Brébeuf first lived among the Montagnais for about a year and learned some of their language. Then, for some 15 years, he lived among the Huron, and he gave their language particular thought. He noted that the Huron used compound words a lot and that they had different verbs for things. He also began to realize the different cultural values in language. For example, he was trying to teach the Christian prayer that begins "Our Father who art in heaven," but discovered that it was very insulting to the Huron to speak of a dead parent. So Brébeuf had to substitute another word for father in order not to give offense. Before he died at the hands of the Huron's enemy, the Iroquois, he had compiled a Catholic catechism (doctrine) in Huron and a French-Huron dictionary.

familiar territory. As Radisson noted, "We mett several sorts of people. We conversed [with] them, being in longtime alliance [with] them." There they heard of a great river that forked with one branch going to the west and the other to the south. Radisson and Groseilliers believed that the great river to the south they heard of "runns towards Mexico from the tokens they gave us." By "tokens," Radisson meant that the gifts the Native Americans gave them were in fact trade goods of European, probably Spanish, origin. The river they were hearing about was the Mississippi.

However, the traders' interests lay not to the south but to the north, in a climate in which animals produce richer furs. The rest of the Frenchmen in their party had turned back, but the two adventurers still had Huron and other local guides and interpreters. Along Lake Superior's shores, they were accompanied by as many as 20 boats of the Anishinabe (Chippewa) people. Radisson recorded, "they keepe us company, in hopes to gett knives from us," an important trade item. Radisson and Groseilliers built a makeshift fort when they got to Chequamegon Bay and enjoyed the fact that they were the first Europeans to see the area. This was probably the same spot where Father Claude Allouez built his mission when he arrived there a few years later.

The two men enjoyed the freedom their adventures offered, however, this sometimes meant that they were also free to suffer. One winter they were reduced to eating the dogs that traveled with them. Another time, when their sleds were laden down with "a great store of booty," Radisson's sled broke through some thin ice. In his efforts to save the load, he injured himself and became soaked with icy water. Groseilliers left him wrapped warmly and rushed off to get help. After running a fever for a week, Radisson slowly regained his strength.

Aided by Native American guides and interpreters, the men ranged into what is now the Mille Lacs region of Minnesota and met the Dakota Indians. Moving north they met the Cree, who occupied territory between Lake Superior and Hudson Bay. All along the way, they not only were able to trade for luxurious glossy furs but heard stories of yet greater riches to the north. They realized the possibility that, given the distance from Montreal, this source of furs might be better tapped from the sea. They returned to Quebec elated and laden with high-quality furs.

Unfortunately, the governor of New France, although delighted at their haul, did not greet them or their plan with open arms. In fact, the two men's plan interfered with his tight control of fur-trade routes. He not only had no interest in sponsoring a sea journey, he fined them for trading without a license.

In response, Radisson and Groseilliers turned to the English. In London, they found merchants willing to sponsor a sea voyage to Hudson Bay. The cargo the ship brought back was so lucrative that their backers immediately formed the Hudson's Bay Company, created by royal charter in 1670. King Charles II gave the company a monopoly over trade. He also gave it the right to govern not only the bay but also all the land draining into it, an area covering 3,036,000 square miles (7,770,000 sq km). Unfortunately, the two Frenchmen did not get to share the wealth their actions generated. The company employed them for five years after its founding, but they ultimately left and returned to New France.

The English, now with posts on Hudson Bay and at Albany, saw the chance to extend their influence into the Ohio River Valley and possibly interfere with French trading networks there. Into this potentially volatile situation, two new figures came to political power in New France. The first of these was a new intendant, Jean Talon, who arrived in Quebec in 1665. The intendant was an official who was responsible for the administration of justice and economic growth. The other, who arrived seven years later, was a new governor, Count Frontenac. In the French imperial system, the governor's primary responsibility was colonial defense.

Frontenac and Talon wanted to secure and add to French claims to the continent. The first important journey of exploration they sponsored was that of Father Jacques Marquette and Louis Jolliet. In the commission that Frontenac and Talon gave them, they expressed hope that the great river they had heard about from the Native Americans might prove to be the elusive route to China or might lead to nations where there were "said to be numerous gold mines." Old dreams die slowly.

As noted earlier, Marquette and Jolliet's party succeeded in reaching the Mississippi, but they decided to end their journey before they reached its mouth. They returned to Lake Michigan by way of the Illinois River, to which Native guides had directed them. Later, Marquette was anxious to return to the Illinois River region to establish a mission, and he set off the following year. By 1675 he was almost there, but unfortunately he died before reaching his goal. Jolliet returned to the St. Lawrence River Valley and never traveled west again.

With Marquette and Jolliet's journey, French claims to the interior of the continent seemed secure. Still, the French knew that the English colonies on the coast were becoming more populous and more economically and militarily secure. A small English presence had arrived around the southern part of Hudson Bay but had yet to make serious inroads into either French fur-trading interests or Native societies. Native Americans continued to adapt to the new economic, political, and cultural world in which they found themselves and, where possible, tried to shape tumultuous events to their own advantage. From the perspective of the English and the French, however, the opening up of new markets around Hudson Bay and along the Illinois and Mississippi rivers just raised the stakes of the competition between them. Both were anxious to explore the territory quickly.

6

La Salle's Adventures and Wartime Misery 1673–1715

IN 1675 RENÉ-ROBERT CAVELIER, SIEUR DE LA SALLE, SET SAIL FROM France to travel to Quebec, the capital of New France. La Salle had received royal support for his plan to establish forts all around the Great Lakes and to become governor of all the territory he might discover between New France and the Spanish-claimed territory of Mexico and Florida. Traveling with him was Father Louis Hennepin, a Récollet priest from Belgium. Hennepin's official duty was to establish a mission in the new territory, but the journey also satisfied his longtime desire to travel. In the book that Hennepin later wrote about his journey, *A New Discovery of a Vast Country in America*, he remembered that, as a young man, he had been so drawn to travel that he used to frequent "victualling-houses [eating places] to hear the seamen give an account of their adventures."

La Salle's expedition gave Hennepin the great adventure he had longed for. In 1678, Hennepin passed Niagara Falls, which he thought the "most terrifying waterfall in the universe." Below the falls, Hennepin watched the construction of a ship, the *Griffon*, that La Salle was having built. In 1679, it was the first sailing ship to navigate the Great Lakes, and it took the expedition to the new French post at Michilimackinac, on the Straits of Mackinac. Here Lakes Huron and Michigan meet. From there, La Salle sent the *Griffon* back with a load of furs, but unfortunately it was never heard from again.

The expedition pressed on. La Salle's second in command, Henri Tonti (sometimes spelled Tonty), located the Chicago River and the portage to the Illinois River, which he knew was the route by which

A Franciscan friar, Louis Hennepin journeyed with Robert de La Salle on his expedition aboard the *Griffon*, the first large ship to sail across the Great Lakes. Hennepin was also the first European to view and describe Niagara Falls and St. Anthony Falls. He published the first engraving of Niagara Falls in his book *Nouvelle Decouverte* (*above*).

Marquette and Jolliet had returned to Lake Michigan from the Mississippi. La Salle's party now followed the route down the Illinois River to near present-day Peoria, Illinois, where they stopped and built Fort Crèvecoeur. La Salle then returned to Quebec to sell the furs they had acquired. While he was gone, he instructed Hennepin and two other Frenchmen to go to the Mississippi River and head north to explore the river's headwaters.

At this point, Hennepin's adventure became more than he had bargained for. Six weeks into their journey, the group was captured by a Dakota war party on its way to attack the Miami and the Illinois Indians. The war party turned around and, with its prisoners, headed home to what is now the Mille Lacs region of Minnesota. It was a difficult journey upstream to near present-day St. Paul. From there, the party walked overland for five days. The captives stayed with the Dakota for four months until they were finally rescued by Daniel Greysolon, sieur Du Luth, a French explorer and a cousin of Henri Tonti's who was exploring west of Lake Superior. After lengthy negotiations between Du Luth and the Dakota, Hennepin and his group were released. Du Luth and his party escorted them back to Michilimackinac, where Hennepin was pleasantly surprised to find a Jesuit priest from his hometown of Ath, Belgium.

EUROPEAN RIVALRIES IN NORTH AMERICA

It was a small European world around the Great Lakes of North America. Throughout the late seventeenth and early eighteenth centuries, a number of traders, explorers, *coureurs de bois* (French Canadian fur trappers), and priests passed through the trading centers at Forts Frontenac (modern Kingston, Ontario) and Michilimackinac on their way to and from the west. At this time, there were probably only a few hundred Frenchmen in the backcountry, but since many of them passed through these trading centers at one time or another, they came to know one another.

These small centers of activity were becoming key parts of great imperial struggles. The journeys of exploration in this period brought Europeans not only new information and alliances with Native American trading partners, but also brought the groups into direct contact in the interior of the continent. Coincidentally, they began bumping into one another at exactly the time their countrymen were coming to blows in Europe. The result was a new anxiety about international competition and more bloodshed when the European wars became North American ones.

La Salle's discoveries during the 1680s were an important part of the increased tension between the French and English over who controlled what land in North America. La Salle returned to the west in 1681 and, the following year, traveled with Tonti and a large party down the Mississippi all the way to the Gulf of Mexico. Tonti had had a grueling time in the Illinois Country while waiting for La Salle to return. In his report of the expedition to his patron, Abbé Renaudot, Tonti told him that the party had been so hungry in winter 1680, they were reduced to eating "acorns which we found under the snow" and had been glad to "feast" on the remains of a deer "which had just been devoured by wolves." On the journey down the Mississippi with La Salle, however, food was plentiful. La Salle wrote later that they found "roes [deer], bears not savage and very good to eat, turkeys and all sorts of game."

LA SALLE'S FATEFUL EXPEDITION

On a successful journey down to the mouth of the Mississippi, La Salle claimed all the territory of the river valley for France, which he named La Louisiane in honor of King Louis XIV, and extended French interests to the edge of the Spanish Empire. Despite this great accomplishment, those who knew him remembered him as unstable. Father René Bréhant de Galinée, who had met La Salle in 1669, described La Salle in his journal as acting "almost in a daze," and others thought him incompetent and bad tempered. However, La Salle was ambitious and driven by the desire to find a route to China. He never found it, but having made the discoveries he had, he was determined to benefit from them. He wanted to found a settlement at the mouth of the Mississippi and govern it. He would not succeed in doing that either, but his actions set in motion another string of related journeys of exploration.

La Salle needed King Louis XIV's approval for this new settlement at the mouth of the Mississippi. He returned to Quebec by retracing his route via the French post at Michilimackinac and then went on to France to get the approval. After receiving permission, he set sail from France in 1684 in four ships and with 320 people to found the colony. Sailing along the coast of the Gulf of Mexico, he could not locate the Mississippi from the sea. Instead, he landed at Matagorda Bay, off the Texas coast. Here he built a fort at Garcitas Creek. By 1687, sickness, desertion, death, and hunger reduced the party to about 36 people.

Setting off overland in search of the Mississippi, he located the Rio Grande and then proceeded across south-central Texas, reaching perhaps as far as the Trinity River. Finally, the party's frustration with La Salle's incompetence, bad temper, and poor planning turned violent. Intrigue and mystery surround the subsequent events, but apparently, in March 1687, the party set upon one another, and La Salle was one of those killed.

Meanwhile, Tonti had heard of La Salle's expedition by sea. In 1686, he led a party from the Great Lakes region down the Mississippi

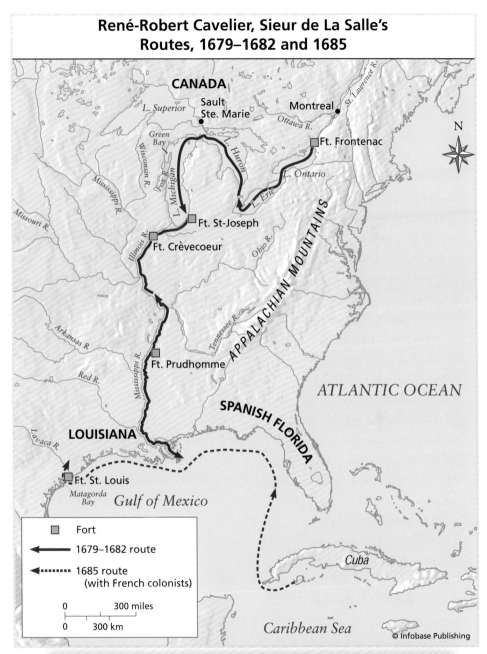

René-Robert Cavelier, Sieur de La Salle's Routes, 1679–1682 and 1685

In 1682, Robert de La Salle canoed down the Mississippi River and claimed the territory around the mouth of the river in the name of France. Two years later, La Salle tried to repeat his successful expedition in order to establish a colony on the Gulf of Mexico, but was unable to relocate the Mississippi.

to look for him. Upon reaching the Gulf Coast, he sent search crews out 60 to 70 miles (96 to 112 km) in each direction, but they had no luck. Tonti returned to New France and, in 1688, was on the Illinois River when he met five men who had been part of La Salle's party. One of them was La Salle's brother, Abbé Jean Cavelier. The men concealed the fact that La Salle was dead, and Abbé Cavelier asked Tonti for a loan to pay for his passage home. The following year, Tonti led another party south to search for rumored survivors but found none. Before returning to New France, he made extensive journeys of exploration up the Red River, often traveling with Jean Couture, a coureur de bois. They reached what is today northeastern Texas.

Abbé Cavelier and the rest of the survivors from the La Salle expedition were making their way back to Canada through Michilimackinac when they met another traveler, Louis-Armand de Lom d'Arce, baron de Lahontan. The previous year, Lahontan had traveled with Du Luth to Fort St. Joseph, which Du Luth had earlier established at the entrance to Lake Huron from Lake Erie. That fort was running short of supplies, and it was a quest for provisions that brought Lahontan to Michilimackinac in 1688. Lahontan later became famous as an explorer largely by writing popular books about his adventures. Ironically, he became most famous for a journey he probably made up. He wrote that he started "another journey because I cannot stand to mope around here [Fort St. Joseph] all winter" and left with five "good Ottawa hunters" and some others. Years later, he described at length a "long river" he had found and the peoples who lived along it. No one else ever found the "long river." The popular books he wrote about his travels were a mixture of interesting fact, cultural and geographical detail, and imagination.

EUROPEAN CONFLICTS SPREAD TO NORTH AMERICA

Adventurers now routinely traveled along the corridor between Michilimackinac and the Mississippi River. Their activities intensified as war broke out in Europe in 1689. That war concerned the European balance of power and, while it involved other nations, it primarily pitted Britain and France against each other. In North America, it was called King William's War and lasted from 1689 to 1697. A second European war, also concerning the balance of power among the leading European states, broke out in 1702. This second war was known in North America as Queen Anne's War and was ended by the Treaty of Utrecht in 1713.

When the first of these wars broke out in 1689, the French decided to attack the English trading posts on Hudson Bay. The French chose Pierre Le Moyne, sieur d'Iberville, a Montreal-born naval officer, to lead the raid. He returned to New France with a large haul of furs and English prisoners and repeated his success the following year. At the end of the war, Iberville moved on to a warmer climate. In 1698, he led an expedition from France to Louisiana by sea, found the mouth of the Mississippi, and explored the delta region. He returned with reinforcements the following year and sent out parties, including one led by his brother Jean-Baptiste Le Moyne, sieur de Bienville, to explore the Pearl River in Mississippi and the Red River in Louisiana. For the moment, Spain and France were allies, and Iberville received assistance from the Spanish in settling colonists on Mobile Bay, in present-day Alabama. With these expeditions, Iberville broke the Spanish monopoly of the Gulf of Mexico.

Joining the Louisiana explorers were some old hands from the Great Lakes. Tonti arrived in 1700, and Iberville used him as a negotiator with the Choctaw and Chickasaw peoples. Pierre Charles Le Sueur, a coureur de bois who had become wealthy trading on Lake Superior, also joined him. Le Sueur had already found a route from Lake Superior to the Mississippi River. Now, in 1700, Le Sueur led a large party up the Mississippi from the coast all the way to just below the St. Anthony Falls (now Minneapolis). They then traveled up the Minnesota River to the Blue Earth River before arriving at a post already established by Nicolas Perrot, a fur trader who was influential in expanding trade, near Lake Pepin, a broad section of the Mississippi where the Chippewa River flows into it. One member of the expedition, André Penicaut, kept a journal. He noted that the French were trading in "pelts and other merchandise" and that "game is very plentiful in the prairies." The party traded with the "Cioux" (Sioux), Penicaut wrote, and had found St. Anthony's Falls, which "one can hear two leagues [about six miles or nine kilometers] away."

Another experienced Great Lakes explorer and fur trader arrived in 1713 to be the new governor of Louisiana. He was Antoine de la Mothe Cadillac, who had commanded Fort Michilimackinac and established Fort Pontchartrain (now Detroit). As governor of Louisiana, he sent out a large number of exploring parties in search of minerals such as lead and copper. One of these parties was led by François Guyon Des Prés Derbanne, who claimed to already have traveled up the Missouri River. He and Louis Juchereau de Saint-Denis, who had come with Iberville, explored many parts of East Texas and reached the Spanish community at San Juan Bautista across the Rio Grande.

THE ENGLISH ROLE

While French government energies were directed toward the Great Lakes, the Mississippi River Valley, and Louisiana, the Englishmen of the Hudson's Bay Company were extending their influence west at higher latitudes. As a rule, the English were reluctant to leave their posts, preferring that the Native Americans brought furs to them. In 1690, Henry Kelsey, a skilled linguist and company employee, was sent off, not to explore specifically but to make new contacts and encourage western Indians to bring their furs into the company post. His journey took him overland farther west than any European had yet gone in the region.

Kelsey set off from Hudson Bay and probably traveled down the Hayes and Fox rivers. They eventually reached the Saskatchewan River near what is now The Pas, Manitoba. He spent the winter there with the Assiniboine and then continued west the following year to present-day Saskatoon. He probably met Sioux (Dakota, Lakota, Nakota) or Atsina (Gros Ventre) Indians on the prairie, traveled with them on bison hunts, and saw a grizzly bear. Little evidence of his exploits survives except a journal that he kept. He wrote it in rhyme, probably to entertain himself. For example, he wrote: "This wood is poplo ridges with small ponds of water/There is beavour in abundance but no otter." After two years, he returned to the company post called York Factory leading "a good fleet of Indians." Decades would pass before another Hudson's Bay Company man went so far west again.

Meanwhile, in the English colonies on the east coast of the Atlantic, population and economic growth was rapid. By 1700, there were about a quarter of a million people living in the colonies. Of this total, about 10 percent were enslaved Africans, most of whom lived around Chesapeake Bay and in the Carolinas. In all of the English colonies, most people still lived close to the coast or near navigable rivers, although the farming frontier was moving slowly inland.

Enterprising souls still vigorously pursued trade with Native Americans, and that activity led them to map new territory. In 1683, Henry Woodward, an agent of the Carolina proprietors, explored westward from coastal South Carolina. He traveled to what is now western Georgia, established trading posts on the middle Chattahoochee River, and began trading with the Creek. He also ran into some opposition from the Spanish, who went looking for him, but Woodward quickly returned to Charleston.

Another enterprising man was Thomas Dongan of New York, who was appointed governor in 1683. He was eager to divert the French fur trade to New York and sponsored a number of journeys west. The first of these, in 1685, was led by Johannes Roseboom (Rooseboom), a Dutch Albany fur trader. Guided by a French army deserter, Abel Merrion, Roseboom led a large party in 10 canoes laden with trade goods. He naturally headed for the place where Native Americans and fur traders congregated, the French fort at Michilimackinac. He traveled down Lake Ontario, portaged to Lake Erie, then on to Lake Huron, where the Ottawa and Huron were eager to trade. French governor Jacques René de Brisay, marquis de Denonville, was outraged when he heard about Roseboom's actions. "Missilimakinak is theirs," he wrote. "They have taken its latitude, have been to trade there with our Outawa and Huron Indians, who received them cordially on account of the bargains they gave." He lamented that there had not been enough Frenchmen at the fort at the time to drive them off. Dongan, on the other hand, was thrilled with the party's success and sent Roseboom out again the following year.

In 1687, Dongan sponsored another venture, this time by Arnold (Arnout) Viele, another Dutch fur trader from Albany and a skilled linguist. He, too, headed for Michilimackinac, but unfortunately the French took him prisoner and held him at Quebec before he finally escaped. In 1692, traveling with Lenni Lenape (Delaware) and Shawnee guides, he went to the Ohio River Valley to trade, probably by way of the Delaware, Susquehanna, and Allegheny rivers.

These trips, England's success in breaking into the French fur trade, and a nasty exchange of letters between the governors of New France and New York happened before the outbreak of King William's War in 1689. This tense environment did not bode well for restraint in war. The

stakes for the Europeans were high. France and England saw an opportunity to drive the other from the continent, and Spain was anxious to
defend its imperial interests. New England troops and their Iroquois
allies fought the French and their Algonquian allies. During the war,
French and Algonquian troops sacked Schenectady, New York, in 1690,
and New England troops seized Port Royal, which was the principal
town in Acadia, in modern-day Nova Scotia. The Treaty of Ryswick that
ended the war in 1697 returned all the territory that either side had
captured in North America.

The next war broke out just as Iberville was establishing his settlement in Louisiana. This time there was fighting in many parts of the colonies. The English attacked the Spanish at St. Augustine and their other
missions in Florida. A joint Spanish and French force attacked Charleston, South Carolina. In 1704, an Abenaki and Mohawk force attacked the
Massachusetts town of Deerfield on the Connecticut River. New England
troops again took Port Royal and kept it under the final peace treaty, the
Treaty of Utrecht, in 1713. The war prompted the Spanish to reinforce its
military presence in Florida, and in 1718 it established permanent settlements at the outer edge of its empire in Texas at San Antonio.

In the midst of this warring, the Iroquois carved out a diplomatic
solution to protect themselves. In 1701, still powerful but weakened by
repeated epidemics, they developed a policy of neutrality. This policy,
combined with their military strength, meant that for the next few
decades the Iroquois were able to play the two major European powers
against each other. This worked because both Great Britain and France
had a vested interest in keeping the Iroquois neutral, at least to prevent
them from allying with the other side and to keep trade goods flowing.

All this activity provided a backdrop for English exploration at the
end of the seventeenth century. War gave an extra motive to Englishmen
anxious to break into the French fur trade. To that end, in 1698, Thomas
Welch of South Carolina set off from Charleston for the Arkansas River.
The following year, William Bond wanted to get to the Gulf Coast and
set off with a large party from Charleston overland to the Mississippi.
They were guided by Jean Couture, who had explored Texas with Tonti
in 1686 in the search for the La Salle party. Bond then traveled down-
river to the Gulf of Mexico and explored the coastline of Florida.

THE VOYAGEURS

Voyageurs were canoe men who worked for a wage and were the force on which the French fur trade rested. They learned their craft from Native Americans. Samuel de Champlain greatly admired the skill of the Native guides as his party navigated falls where there were dangerous "eddies and surf." He noted that the guides navigated these "with the greatest possible dexterity, winding about and going by the easiest places, which they recognize at a glance." The French voyageurs had to learn this skill and build up stamina. Men paddled for hours at a time, setting the pace with songs, and paddling at about 45 strokes per minute. Heavily laden as they were with trade goods or furs, portages were difficult. Everything had to be removed from the canoes and carried past rapids, a waterfall, or to another waterway, and then the canoes had to be carried. Occasionally, the voyageurs might run rapids, letting the turbulent, fast-moving water carry them, but that meant risking the precious cargo of furs if they should spill and, possibly, risking their lives. When they were traveling against the flow of a river, the going was tough. Sometimes in difficult terrain, to avoid a portage, the men towed their canoes, either wading in the cold water or walking along the river's edge. It was a hard life, but the men who did it enjoyed their independence and celebrated their strength and endurance in their own stories and songs.

The next year, Couture was instrumental in helping other Carolinian traders break the French hold on the fur trade on the Mississippi. Few Europeans knew more about the region than Couture. After Couture's previous travel with Tonti, he traveled on the Ohio and Tennessee rivers, traded with the Cherokee, and traveled to Spanish posts in Florida before arriving in Charleston. He was thus able to lead Carolinian traders along the Savannah, Tennessee, and Ohio rivers to the Mississippi.

Couture was not the only French fur trader to work and settle with the English. Others were instrumental in extending English influence in the fur trade in the new English colony of Pennsylvania. Founded by the wealthy English Quaker William Penn in 1681, its European population soared, reaching almost 20,000 within 20 years. Most of its settlers farmed, but a number, including Penn's agent James Logan, wanted to break into the French fur trade. They did not explore themselves but simply hired French fur traders who knew the region. Pierre Bisaillon was one of them. He, too, had been with Tonti on the 1686 search party. Now with Martin Chartier and Jacques Le Tort, he provided most of the furs for Logan, bringing them in to posts established on the Susquehanna River. Of course, being French during wars against France sometimes meant that Bisaillon was harassed by local English officials. Logan came to his defense, writing that Bisaillon, "though a Frenchman, he had been very faithful."

In Virginia, the lieutenant governor, Alexander Spotswood, was also eager to enter the fur trade and promote westward settlement. He sponsored journeys to the Blue Ridge range searching for a route to the Great Lakes. In 1716, he led a group of gentlemen, their servants, rangers, and Native American guides along the Rapidan River in northern Virginia and then overland to the Shenandoah River. He formally claimed the Shenandoah Valley of northwestern Virginia for England and returned home and promoted it as a perfect place for Englishmen to settle.

CONFLICTS WITH NATIVE AMERICANS

English exploration and expanding settlement led to a new round of battles with Native Americans. By 1710, there were so many English settlers along the South Carolina coast down to the Savannah River that tensions rose with the local Yamassee and Creek Indians. War broke out in 1716, and both groups were defeated by the English and their Cherokee allies.

Earlier, in North Carolina, tensions between mostly Swiss and German settlers and the Tuscarora also had led to the Tuscarora War of 1711–1713. The plight of the Tuscarora demonstrates some of the complications Native Americans faced as they encountered Europeans. Once powerful, their numbers had declined from disease, and they had suffered at the hands of their more powerful Native American neighbors

King Charles granted a charter to William Penn, which made Penn the largest private landowner in the New World. Penn proclaimed that the English colony, which would later be named Pennsylvania, would not exploit the Native Peoples or immigrants. Pictured above, Penn informs Native Americans of his intentions to establish an English colony there.

who were allied with Virginian and Carolinian traders. Finally, the Tuscarora struck back, attacking a European settlement. The colonists responded with a devastating attack that killed hundreds of Tuscarora. Others were captured and sold into slavery. The remainder, perhaps about 2,000, moved north and sought protection from the powerful Iroquois. In 1722, they were admitted as the sixth nation in the Iroquois Confederacy, although not on equal terms with the original five nations.

THE FRENCH REASSERT THEMSELVES

This flurry of English competition on the Mississippi and its tributary rivers did not distract the French from exploring new territory. In fact, it gave their explorations a new urgency. Additionally, the peace treaty that marked the end of Queen Anne's War specifically required France to acknowledge Britain's right to Hudson Bay. This meant there could be no more attacks against the English there to drive them out of the market.

If the French were to remain dominant in the fur trade, however, they had to make new contacts with people who trapped the animals that bore the luxuriant furs found in cold climates. So the French government authorized the governor of New France, Philippe de Rigaud, marquis de Vaudreuil, to send expeditions westward from the Great Lakes and the Mississippi River Valley. Vaudreuil was eager to comply. He was a military officer who had been involved in campaigns against the Iroquois and was experienced in working with Native allies. He thought it critical to increase French control of the western fur trade. The new French plan was for the government to pay for the expeditions, but the forts established would be self-supporting from their fur-trading activities. With this plan, the French government explicitly linked the fur trade to its national interests. And, by the end of the decade, a new wave of explorers were heading into what is today Minnesota and Manitoba.

By the end of this period, the French laid claim to the Ohio and Mississippi river valleys by means of a system of forts and missions but with a scant population. The Spanish, too, maintained a tenuous hold on Florida and Texas, the outposts of its empire. Meanwhile, the population of the English colonies was rising rapidly, and adventurers and traders from the middle and southern colonies were now regular visitors to the Mississippi. The stage was set for another century of new discoveries and new conflicts for Europeans and native peoples.

7

Gaining Knowledge and Coming to Blows 1715–1783

IN 1749 FRENCH JESUIT PRIEST FATHER JOSEPH-PIERRE de Bonnecamps was on an expedition to what he called "La Belle Rivière," the Beautiful River. This was one of the names the French gave to the Upper Ohio River. The expedition was led by Pierre Joseph Céleron de Blainville, an army officer whom Bonnecamps greatly admired. The goal of the expedition was to map and secure French claims to the Ohio River Valley.

The party of about 200 Frenchmen, Native guides, and interpreters set off in 23 canoes from Montreal. On their journey, they had some exhausting portages. Bonnecamps noted that Céleron regularly needed "to give his people a breathing space." The party was traveling in late July, so the rivers had low water levels. This caused the party even more hard work. Céleron was so despondent about it that, when they came to low water on the Chautauqua River, Bonnecamps wrote, "a fatal hour, which plunged us again into our former miseries." They were forced to "the sad necessity" of dragging the canoes over the stones in the riverbed.

Despite this occasional misery, Bonnecamps was a keen observer of the world around him. He measured the latitude regularly and carefully noted the plants and animals. He was excited to see his first rattlesnake. He had heard that, if a person was bitten, a "sovereign remedy" was to apply a mixture of saliva and sea salt. He was pleased to note, though, that the party had not had "any occasion to put this antidote to the test."

The expedition staked its claim to the region by walking around it. The party traveled out by way of Lake Ontario and Lake Erie. They portaged over to the Allegheny River, then traveled along the Ohio to the Great Miami River near what is now Cincinnati. Then they returned to Montreal by Fort des Miamis (present-day Fort Wayne, Indiana). Along the route, Céleron buried lead plates. These plates signified "the renewal of possession which we [the French] have taken of the said river Ohio and of all those [rivers] which fall into it, of all lands on both sides of it as far as the sources of said streams."

At first, the expedition appeared to have been a success. Céleron had ordered some Englishmen who were trading with the Native Americans to leave the area, and they did. Since trading and military relationships were closely connected, the French were particularly anxious to prevent the British from making these trade connections. Having sent the Englishmen away, Céleron tried to arrange alliances with the Native Peoples he met to secure their loyalty to France.

Still, the expedition ultimately failed. The Englishmen, who were trading for bear, otter, and deer skins, came back as soon as Céleron's party left. They succeeded in drawing Native communities into their trading networks. Despite Céleron's efforts to reinforce loyalty, French fur traders often were not very interested in trading there. They could make much more money in colder climates. In lands far to the north and west, more luxuriant furs were to be found. So even though the French knew the military importance of the Ohio River Valley, they did not do enough to strengthen their trading networks there. Tension increased between the British and French in the region. In time it led to bloodshed, with Native Americans caught in the middle.

However, for most of the first half of the eighteenth century, British and French explorers usually managed to stay out of each other's way. The French explored the rich fur-trading territory west of the Great Lakes and the territory west of Louisiana that is present-day Texas. British explorers and settlers moved steadily inland from their coastal communities toward the Appalachians. In the 40 years between signing the Treaty of Utrecht that ended Queen Anne's War in 1713 until conflict began in the Ohio River Valley in 1754, British and French traders greatly added to European knowledge of North America.

European Possessions in North America, 1713

In the first half of the eighteenth century, British and French explorers stayed out of each other's territory. The French claimed the territory west of the Great Lakes. The British controlled the coastal communities in the east. The Spanish claimed New Spain (present-day Mexico and Central America). Soon conflict developed when the colonists began to claim the same territories.

THE FRENCH PUSH WESTWARD

In the early 1700s, the first focus of the French explorers was the area immediately to the west of Lake Superior, particularly Rainy Lake, in present-day southwestern Ontario, on the border with Minnesota. In 1717 the governor of New France, Philippe de Rigaud, marquis de Vaudreuil, sponsored an expedition there led by Zacharie Robutel de la Noüe. The cold climate in the region promised good quality furs. The French hoped they could encourage western Native Americans not to trade with the Hudson's Bay Company. They also still hoped to find a river route to the western sea and China.

Robutel set out with a large party. He wanted to establish several trading posts. He managed to set up a post on the Kaministikwia River. This river flows into the north side of Lake Superior. However, he probably got no farther west. He found himself in the middle of hostilities between the Dakota and the Cree. After four years, he returned home to Montreal.

The driving energy for the next push westward came from the La Vérendrye family. Pierre Gaultier de Varennes, sieur de La Vérendrye, was an enthusiastic adventurer. He had heard tales of a great river leading to the western sea. In 1731, La Vérendrye set off with his sons, a nephew, and 50 men. By the following year, they had built a fort at the Lake of the Woods. This lake lies at the border of present-day Ontario, Minnesota, and Manitoba. He set up another fort at Lake Winnipeg. Relations between the Dakota and the Cree were still tense. La Vérendrye avoided the conflict for a while; however, in 1736, about 21 of his men, including one of his sons, were killed, probably by the Dakota. Still, La Vérendrye was determined to stay.

By 1738, he had ventured farther west. The Assiniboine people guided him across the prairies. He was impressed by these "magnificent plains of three or four leagues in extent." He also was impressed by the Assiniboine. They moved in a column with advance scouts. Guards watched the sides and rear. The weakest members of the community traveled in the middle.

The party journeyed across the plains and reached the headwaters of the Missouri River. There they met the Mandan people. La Vérendrye had been eager to question the Mandan about a river route to the western sea; however, he could not speak the Mandan language. This left the party "reduced to trying to make ourselves understood by signs and gestures." The expedition was forced to return home.

In 1742, two of La Vérendrye's sons set off and met the Mandan again. This time, they set off to the west with Mandan guides. By January 1743, they reached mountains, probably the Big Horn Mountains in northern Wyoming. They also met Cheyenne and Pawnee peoples along the way. As with Céleron, these explorers also buried a lead plate. The plate marked French claims to what is today Pierre, South Dakota.

The French also were busy exploring lands west of the Mississippi. In 1714, French officer Claude Charles Dutisné traveled through Illinois Country. He reached the Mississippi, then traveled south to Louisiana. Two years later, he traveled up the Red River, setting up a post named for the peoples who lived there, the Natchitoches. In 1719, the governor of Louisiana, Jean-Baptiste Le Moyne, sieur de Bienville, sponsored him to travel up the Missouri River. On that journey he met the Osage and the Pawnee.

Other French explorers were busy in the area, too. François Guyon des Prés Derbanne was on the Red River the same year as Dutisné. Derbanne lived on Dauphin Island on Mobile Bay. He set off with a group of traders by canoe. They reached the Natchitoches post. From there, they went by land on mules to what is now eastern Texas. They spent two months trading with the Hasinai people. Derbanne even crossed the Rio Grande to the Spanish fort and mission at San Juan Bautista, Mexico. Derbanne decided there was not enough money to be made trading there and settled in Natchitoches with his wife, Jeanne. She was probably a Natchitoches Indian.

THE BRITISH EXPLORE THE WEST

While the French were exploring toward the west, so were the English traders from the Hudson's Bay Company. For a long time they had been content to stay at their posts on the bay and let the Native American hunters make the long journey to them to sell their furs. The French journeys westward changed their minds. The company now wanted to make direct contact with the nations to the west of the Cree, mainly the Atsina (Gros Ventre) and nations of the Blackfoot confederacy.

The man chosen to forge these new relationships was Anthony Henday. He set off in June 1754 from York Factory, the Hudson's Bay Company trading post on the western side of the bay at the mouth of the Nelson River. He was traveling with a party of Cree, who were returning west after selling their furs at the post. When they got to the prairies, the expedition left their canoes and the rivers behind and went by land, crossing Saskatchewan and reaching what is today the Battleford area.

On his journey, Henday traded with Assiniboine people. On October 18, 1754, he arrived in a Blackfoot village near present-day Red Deer, Alberta, with the Cree fur trader Ateesh-Ka-Sees, Henday's guide and interpreter. Although the Blackfoot greeted them warmly, the community's leaders were not willing to make the difficult journey to Hudson's Bay to sell their furs. The French Fort Pasquia (now The Pas, Manitoba) was much easier to get to. Henday observed in his journal, that French traders "talk several languages to perfection." Thus he felt that the French "have the advantage of us in every shape."

Henday pushed farther west and may have been the first European to see the Rocky Mountains. In spring 1755, he began the journey home. On his way, he came across another French trading post, and Henday noted that he and the Frenchmen met each other with "a good deal of Bowing and Scraping, but neither he understood me nor I him." In the next five years, Henday made several more trips to the west before he left the company's service.

Like the French, British explorers also stayed active west and east of the Mississippi River. Mark Catesby traveled around South Carolina beginning in 1722. He made detailed notes and drawings of plants as he explored along the Savannah River. He passed through Georgia and into northern Florida. John Brickell was an Irishman traveling in North Carolina. He set off with 10 other people to travel west through North Carolina to Tennessee. He was interested in what he called the small "rotten-wood worm." He also wanted to learn about the large polecat and buffalo.

THE BRITISH INCREASE ACTIVITY

The end of another war between the British and the French brought new energy to exploration in North America. The war, known in the colonies as King George's War, had lasted from 1744 to 1748. Like the earlier wars, it was mainly fought in Europe with only small battles in North America. After the war, the British Crown granted charters to new land companies in the Ohio River Valley and in Kentucky. This was territory the French also claimed. It was also land which the Native Americans still controlled. The stage was set for renewed exploration and conflict.

One of the earliest explorers in Kentucky was John Findley. He was a British trader who had gone there in 1744. Findley had traded and lived among the Shawnee for many years. He spoke their language. They told him stories of the land of Kanta-Ke. The land there had natural salt springs. These springs attracted grazing animals. Many Native American groups hunted there. It was a perfect place, Findley thought, to establish a trading post.

In 1748, he returned to Virginia. He told Thomas Walker, a wealthy doctor and adventurer, about the rich land to the west. Guided by Findley, Walker and a group of others went in search of it. They crossed a gap in the Allegheny Mountains in what is today eastern Tennessee. Walker named it the Cumberland Gap, after the duke of Cumberland, who was a famous British military leader. Walker circled back to Virginia through southeastern Kentucky by way of the Licking River and the Big Sandy River. This route and the rich hunting grounds were densely forested, and so his overall impression of the region was that it was not suitable for farming. It was about 15 years later before he discovered the fertile lowlands of central Kentucky. However, Walker's report was glowing enough to send many traders into the region and for Virginian investors to organize the Loyal Land Company. In 1749, the company received a royal charter to 800,000 acres (323,748 hectares) in the area that is today southwestern Virginia and southeastern Kentucky.

The real focus of British exploration in this period was the Ohio River Valley. Pennsylvanian traders had been active in the area since the beginning of the century, building geographic knowledge and establishing important trading and political ties. The next great British journey of exploration in the Ohio River Valley was only one year after the French explorer Blainville had buried lead plates to secure France's claim to it. In 1750 Christopher Gist, a trader, was hired by the Ohio Company. Wealthy Virginians owned this land company. They included the family of young George Washington, the future American president. The company had received its royal charter to about 200,000 acres (80,937 ha) of land between the Blue Ridge Mountains and the Ohio River the year before.

Gist's mission was to determine the best route for settlers, describe the best lands, and observe Native American trading patterns. He traveled from Shannopin's Town (named after a famous Delaware Indian chief and located in or near present-day Pittsburgh, Pennsylvania) to

In 1775, frontiersman Daniel Boone led a group through the Cumberland Gap (*shown above*) to widen the path in order to make settlement by pioneers easier. Thousands of settlers followed him through the Cumberland Gap to settle in the West.

the falls of the Ohio River at what is today Louisville, Kentucky, with many side trips up rivers that flow into the Ohio, such as the Scotio and the Muskingum. In his report to the Ohio Company, Gist made useful observations about the landscape. On the Muskingum River, for example, he noted that there were "Meadows upon the Creek, [and] fine Runs for Mills." In another place he noted where the party was in "broken country" and found themselves "cutting our Way thro' a Laurel Thicket." But mostly, Gist found the land fertile and the hunting good.

FRENCH-BRITISH CONFLICT

The French were not going to give up the Ohio River Valley without a fight. The British and the French prepared to challenge each other for the region, and Native Americans were forced to choose sides. The Iroquois chose the British because of their long history of trade. Most other Native Americans sided with the French because the French only wanted to trade and would not settle the land.

The crisis escalated in 1754 when the governor of Virginia sent a military force under a young George Washington into the region to challenge the French. Washington quickly built Fort Necessity near the French Fort Duquesne. After Washington led an unsuccessful attack on Fort Duquesne, the French responded and destroyed Fort Necessity, killing one third of Washington's men. These attacks began the French

FLINTLOCK MUSKETS

Few explorers, adventurers, or traders set off without a flintlock musket. The flintlock musket was the most important weapon used in warfare and hunting in the eighteenth century and thus was a desirable trade item. (Rifles differ from muskets in having "rifled," or spirally grooved, bores.) Muskets had been around since the sixteenth century. In the eighteenth century, the invention of the new flintlock firing mechanism made them safer to use. The new muskets were faster to load and also were more reliable in wet or windy weather. To fire one, users had to complete several steps. They had to put powder in the "priming pan" near the barrel. They had to click a steel plate in place to cover it. Then they had to use a ramrod to push more powder, wadded paper, and the musket ball down the barrel. After removing the ramrod, they could pull the trigger. If this was all done correctly, pulling the trigger would strike the cock containing flint against the steel cover of the pan, igniting the powder in the pan. The powder ignited the main charge, sending the musket ball out the barrel.

Needless to say, a lot could go wrong. The charge might not have been rammed home tightly enough, or the powder might be damp. There might be a "flash in the pan," where the powder in the pan would spark but not ignite the main charge. Still, a well-trained soldier could fire up to four times a minute. This improved firing mechanism made the musket easier to use but not more accurate. The user still could not be sure of hitting any target more than 100 yards (91 meters) away.

and Indian War, which in 1756 merged into a larger war between the British and French, called the Seven Years' War. Unlike earlier wars, this one mostly would be fought in northeastern North America, and at stake was control of the northeast of the continent.

Little exploration took place during the costly and terrible war. When it formally ended in 1763 with the Treaty of Paris, France had lost and Britain was now the sole imperial power in the region. A number of British colonists and traders were excited by the opportunities this presented. They once again turned their sights westward.

DANIEL BOONE EXPLORES

In 1769, the Pennsylvania-born Daniel Boone, a hunter and frontiersman, led a party into Kentucky. He thought he might settle in this new land. He had tried to get there before on a 1767 trip across the Appalachians to hunt with his brother, Squire, and a friend. The hunting had been good, but they were unable to reach the fertile part of Kentucky they had heard about because they were caught in snowstorms. He set off again accompanied by John Findley, his brother-in-law John Stewart, and three other neighbors.

The three leaders of the group had a lot of backcountry experience. Findley was the oldest and had been trading for years in Kentucky. Boone, about 35 years old, was a hunter who had fought in a war against the Cherokee in 1761. John Stewart had been on an earlier expedition with Boone. He also had hunted west of the Appalachians.

The party made their way quickly over the Appalachians. They then passed through the Cumberland Gap. Finally they made their camp at what is today Irvine, Kentucky. After hunting, Boone and Stewart were taken prisoner by the Shawnee, who were appalled to find them hunting on their land. Fortunately, the Shawnee wanted only to warn them off. Boone's nephew, Daniel Boone Bryan, later told an interviewer that the Shawnee treated his uncles in "the most friendly manner." The group escaped and made their way back to camp.

Despite the Shawnee's warning, Boone had seen enough of Kentucky to keep him in the region. In 1770, Boone and Stewart were joined by Boone's brother, Squire, and a friend, Alexander Neeley. The four camped near the present-day town of Blue Lick. Stewart, unfortunately, went missing and was presumed dead. Others found his remains five years later. Neeley returned home, leaving Daniel and Squire Boone to continue to hunt. Soon short of food and ammunition, Squire went home to get more supplies. Daniel was alone for three months. During that time, he wandered Kentucky and became more familiar with the area than any other European.

Daniel Boone's adventures were the subject of books even in his lifetime. Tales of his adventures, often exaggerated by biographers and promoters of Kentucky Country, caused thousands of settlers to follow him through the Cumberland Gap.

PONTIAC'S REBELLION AND THE OHIO RIVER VALLEY

Britain was now the uncontested European power in northeastern North America. With French authority removed, British colonists began to head across the Appalachians. However, the war made the Ohio and Kentucky regions less safe for explorers and settlers. It also dramatically changed relations with Native Peoples. The Iroquois Confederacy had previously enjoyed a powerful position, playing the French and British against each other. Now, with the French gone, they were in a significantly weaker position. As these diplomatic patterns broke down, violence increased, especially in areas where settlers began arriving in increasing numbers.

No one felt this change more keenly than Pontiac, the leader of the Ottawa. Pontiac was a former French ally who lived in western Ohio. In 1763, he led the Ohio peoples in battles against the British in the West. They destroyed a number of forts and attacked the British at Detroit and Fort Pitt (in present-day Pittsburgh). The British were able to defeat Pontiac, whose forces were weakened by military losses and disease, but were shocked at what it cost in lives and money.

To calm the situation, the British government in London issued a proclamation forbidding colonists from settling west of the Appalachians. Its goal was to slow down the westward flow of settlers while British authorities purchased land from Native Americans. This legal barrier, which the colonists called the Proclamation Line, was often ignored.

ACTIVITY IN THE GREAT LAKES REGION

While the Ohio River Valley and the Kentucky Country were the focus of eastern exploration, settlement, and conflict, the fort at

Unhappy with new British policies, Ottawa chief Pontiac arranged a council meeting with ally tribes. Although more than 900 warriors from half a dozen tribes laid siege against British forts Detroit and Pitt, Pontiac's forces were weakened by military losses and disease.

Michilimackinac (at the tip of Michigan where Lake Huron joins Lake Michigan) was again becoming a center of exploring activity. The British fort had been attacked during Pontiac's uprising but now the region was quiet. In 1766 Robert Rogers, a New Hampshire man, was put in command of the fort. He was still convinced, as were others, that there was an inland northwest passage. This was the elusive river route to the Pacific. Rogers sponsored two expeditions to search for it.

The first, in 1766, was led by James Tute. Tute was supposed to make his way to the Saskatchewan River and search for the connecting river from there; however, he traveled no farther than the northwestern edge of Lake Superior. There he was stopped at the Grand Portage. This was the longest portage fur traders had to make in their journey westward. There, Tute heard from Rogers that he had no money to buy supplies for him, so Tute turned back.

Jonathan Carver led the second expedition. Rogers hired Carver to map British territory in the region. French fur traders led Carver to Green Bay. Next, he was guided by the Winnebago people to the Mississippi. He then traveled up the Mississippi to St. Anthony's Falls, modern-day Minneapolis. This territory was previously known only to Native Peoples and the French. He spent the winter with the Dakota Sioux. Carver later wrote of his travels that this was a region that "exceeds for pleasantness and richness of soil all the places that ever I have seen."

The following year, in 1767, Carver met Tute on the Mississippi. Tute had been sent out again to find a river to the Pacific. Together they searched through what is now Wisconsin. At Grand Portage, they again learned that Rogers had no money to supply them. They made their way back to Michilimackinac.

THE FOUNDING OF THE NORTH WEST COMPANY

After the Seven Years' War ended in 1763, individual British traders wanted to make money for themselves. They joined French fur traders in the Far West. Exploring these new lands and finding new sources of fur was appealing for all of them.

These men, with their Native guides and trading partners, dramatically extended geographic knowledge of northwestern North America. The Hudson's Bay Company called them peddlers, that is traveling salesmen who went from place to place buying and selling goods. The company, of course, preferred to have its employees stay in a couple of important posts and have Native hunters come to them with furs. At first, the new traders worked independently, but they soon realized that if they worked together, they could offer more goods at better prices.

In 1783, they started the North West Company. It would challenge the Hudson's Bay Company at every step.

The traders made many important journeys. One of their greatest journeys was made by Peter Pond. In 1778, he traveled through the waterways of the Saskatchewan and Churchill rivers to the Athabasca region. This land stretches across the northernmost parts of modern Saskatchewan and Alberta. Pond discovered an important new portage. It was longer than the Grand Portage at Lake Superior. This one, 13 miles (20.9 km) long, went from Lac La Loche (Methy Lake today) over to the Clearwater River. This new portage opened up a whole new section of the continent to European traders. Pond set up his trading post just south of Lake Athabasca and traded with Cree and Chipewyan hunters. By doing so, he cut off the Hudson's Bay Company's supply of prime furs.

THE HUDSON'S BAY COMPANY RESPONDS

The Hudson's Bay Company also saw the need to expand its operations. At first it set its sights north. The company heard stories of northern copper deposits, still richer furs, and a possible northwest passage. The company hired 24-year-old Samuel Hearne to find these things. He made three journeys between 1769 and 1772. The first ended quickly when his native guides left him and took his supplies. In 1770, he set off again with a large Chipewyan group. He traveled farther, but again, his guides left him.

In 1771, Hearne left for the third time with Matonabbee and his extended family of wives and children. His journey took him to the Coppermine River, which they followed to the Arctic Ocean. He reached Coronation Gulf in July. Looking at the ice-covered water, he realized that no ship would ever be able to get through. If there was a northwest passage, this was not it. His return journey took him a year. When they returned home, he had covered approximately 3,500 miles (5,632 km).

Despite these great journeys, the Hudson's Bay Company and its employees, such as Hearne, still resisted the idea that they should take goods out and peddle them. After Hearne went on to establish the company's first post inland, Cumberland House on the Saskatchewan River in 1773, he was quite clear that Native Americans had to come to him to trade. He wrote in his journal that Native Americans from "Buffalow Country," who had brought in wolf skins, tried to get him to come into their territory, as there were people there who were "desirous of having goods brought as near their own doors as Possable." Hearne told them that his intent was to have the post serve a large community and that policy was "firmly fixed."

A REVOLUTION'S IMPACT ON EXPLORATION

In 1775, war broke out between Britain and the colonists in the colonies along the east coast of North America. During the American Revolution, from 1775 to 1783, settlement in the West was slow, but the war brought a great many men into the region when the Americans were fighting Native Americans who were British allies. Many Native Peoples, especially the Iroquois, felt that the British were the only force holding back American settlement. In 1779, Patriot general John Sullivan led battles against the Iroquois in upstate New York. One soldier, Sergeant Thomas Roberts of New Jersey, wrote in his journal that he saw "the Back Woods" for the first time. He was struck by the good timber he saw and "a piece of Meddo [meadow]" that was very fertile. A number of Revolutionary War soldiers saw opportunity and settled on the frontier after the war.

Exploration continued while the war was going on. Thomas Walker surveyed the boundary between the new states of Virginia and North Carolina in 1779 and 1780. At the time, both states claimed all territory as far as the Mississippi. Walker was unable to get all the way there. He had to estimate the last part.

The result of the American Revolution was the birth of the United States of America. The last few decades had witnessed many important journeys of exploration. These were closely connected to the changes in the political landscape. As the century came to a close, the international stakes stayed high. Britain, Spain, and the United States were the leading powers in North America. Russia was also taking an interest in the continent. American traders and land speculators looked west. The Hudson's Bay Company and the new North West Company tried to outdo each other. The search to find a route to the Pacific only intensified.

8

Exploration at the Turn of the Century
1783–1800

THE YEAR 1797 WAS A GOOD ONE FOR DAVID THOMPSON. THAT YEAR, he left his long-time job at the Hudson's Bay Company to work for its rival fur-trading firm, the North West Company. He wanted to explore, and his new company was glad to let him do it. He set off into the West, determined to take exact measurements of familiar places. He also hoped to find shortcuts for known routes and to find Native American hunters to trade with.

Thompson was well prepared for this trip. He had been apprenticed to the Hudson's Bay Company at age 14. After a few years in Canada, he had traveled on the North Saskatchewan River; wintered with Pie-gan Indians on the Bow River; been tutored in navigation by Philip Turnor, the company's chief surveyor; and survived a life-threatening injury. When his apprenticeship was over at age 21, he was a seasoned backwoodsman.

Thompson's 1797 trip was remarkable. He traveled from Grand Portage through Rainy Lake, Lake of the Woods, Lake Winnipeg, and Lake Winnipegosis. He then followed a series of smaller rivers and lakes that eventually took him to the source of the Assiniboine River, then to the Red Deer River and its source. He finally reached a friend's house on the Souris River in present-day North Dakota. He could have stayed the winter. Instead, he decided to press on. He wanted to meet the Mandan people, who lived on the Missouri River, to encourage them to trade with him.

In early December, he set off across the plains to the section of the Missouri River known as Lake Sakakawea, also in North Dakota.

He now traveled with nine men, one of whom spoke Mandan fluently. They traveled with 30 sled dogs that Thompson thought were "half dog, half wolf." Early in their journey, the temperatures were below freezing. It was "too cold to proceed," Thompson noted, and they stayed in their tents. Moving again, they found themselves in "a perfect storm," with snow blinding them. One man and his team of dogs went missing. After some time, they heard the man's call. They found him crawling in the snow. His dogs and sled were never seen again. The group endured periods when they were all "very hungry, and the dogs getting weak." They eventually reached the Mandan at the end of December. Although they were friendly to the travelers, the Mandan did not want to travel north through the territory of their enemy, the Dakota, just to trade. Thompson and his party returned home after a couple of weeks.

Native Americans would trade fur pelts for European-made goods like weaponry, fish hooks, cloth, and jewelry. Competition increased as furs became harder to find. Spain, Russia, Britain, and France all wanted to control the market. Pictured, deer hide rests on a sapling frame to be tanned.

THE FUR TRADE HEATS UP

Thompson had a long career as a trader and explorer. He traveled over much of the northern part of North America. He and other traders helped map and remap much of the northwest at the end of the eighteenth century.

Traders explored to find new sources of furs because competition between them was increasing. Fur-bearing animals were becoming fewer in regions closer to eastern markets. Traders had to go farther and farther west or north to make new contacts with Native hunters from whom they obtained the furs.

As competition was increasing and furs were getting harder to find, the market was expanding. News of the travels of British, Spanish, and Russian seamen in what is now Oregon and British Columbia sparked interest in trading furs, especially sea otter skins, between the west coast of North America and China. They sailed around Cape Horn—the tip of South America—up the west coast and then across the Pacific. The Russians traded in the northwest from their posts in Alaska and the Kamchatka Peninsula on the western side of the Bering Sea.

It was becoming clear that the Far West would be a source of wealth for traders. However, it was not clear which nation would control it. Spain claimed all land between the Mississippi and the Pacific. It wanted to include the territory north of California and south of Alaska. However, the Spanish claim was weak because the Russians and the British were already there. The race was on to explore and claim the Far West.

THE UNITED STATES AND EXPLORATION

By the end of the eighteenth century, the government of the new United States had not yet participated in exploration. The Treaty of Paris that ended the American Revolution gave the United States control over the land between the Appalachians and the Mississippi. The new government focused on securing that land and creating a stable economy. It wanted to sell land east of the Mississippi to settlers quickly to pay off the national war debt. In 1784, 1785, and 1787, Congress passed three acts called Northwest Ordinances. Here, the "northwest" referred to the area that would become Ohio, Indiana, Illinois, Michigan, Wisconsin, and part of Minnesota. These acts provided for the orderly settlement of the land and set out a way for a territory to become a state and be admitted to the Union. Exploration of the Far West could wait.

Native Americans, of course, had not been part of the peace negotiations ending the Revolutionary War. They had not agreed to their land becoming part of the United States. As the trickle of settlers onto their lands became a flood, violent conflict increased in what was by now the Ohio, Indiana, and Illinois territories. In 1790 and 1791, Little Turtle of the Shawnee led a group of Native Americans and defeated U.S. military forces in the region. The United States sent out a new larger force. In fact, at what is today Fort Recovery in western Ohio, on the banks of the Wabash River, they inflicted on General Arthur St. Clair one of the heaviest military defeats in U.S. history. There, 900 men out of St. Clair's force of about 1,500 were either killed or wounded. The United States sent out a new larger force under General Anthony Wayne, a hero of the American Revolution. In 1794 it defeated Little Turtle's forces at the Battle of Fallen Timbers near present-day Toledo, Ohio. The following year, both sides agreed to the Treaty of Greenville. Under the agreement, the Native Americans gave up most of Ohio and part of Indiana. In return, they were promised a lasting boundary between the United States and their lands.

Farther south, in the 1780s, settlers moved into the land west of Georgia and the Carolinas. It was controlled by the Creek, Cherokee, Choctaw, and Chickasaw. Those peoples also negotiated treaties with the United States and exchanged land for a guarantee of their boundaries. However, settlement there moved at a slower pace than in the north.

At this time, few in the United States focused on new explorations in the Far West. Most saw plenty to do in the new lands between the Appalachians and the Mississippi. Men such as John Sevier, who had been a trader in Tennessee, found opportunity for leadership. He helped organize territory south of the Ohio River and was the first governor of the state of Tennessee after it was admitted to the Union in 1796.

Others such as Daniel Boone preferred the frontier. Boone had served two terms in the Virginia legislature, but he was restless. He had led parties of settlers to Kentucky. However, he never wanted to live surrounded by other families. After the American Revolution, he lived in western Virginia, then on the Ohio River, and later back in Kentucky.

Finally, in 1799, he relocated his family to the Missouri River, which was Spanish-controlled territory. He moved to Femme Osage, about 70 miles (112 km) up the Missouri from the trading center of St. Louis. There he was able to renew his old hunting life.

THE MISSISSIPPI VALLEY AND THE MISSOURI RIVER

St. Louis was attracting settlers who wanted to participate in the vigorous trading life of the town. By 1800 there were just under 2,500 people in and around the town. And, as suited a town at the junction of three rivers—the Mississippi, the Missouri, and the Illinois—it was a diverse community. It included French, Spanish, Métis (people of mixed ancestry), Native Americans, and, slowly, a few U.S. farmers and traders. They were all expanding their activities farther and farther up the Missouri River.

Rumors that traders from Canada already were trading with the Mandan on the Upper Missouri encouraged some traders to push even farther up the river. One of the earliest traders to do so was Jacques d'Église in 1792. He was followed a year later by Jean-Baptiste Truteau, who had been hired by a group of St. Louis merchants. They formed the Company of Explorers of the Upper Missouri. Truteau probably reached the point on the Missouri where the Grand River flows into it and traded with the Arikara people. Truteau passed the Niobrara River and wrote that the river might be "the most abundant one in the entire continent of beaver and otter." Unfortunately, the river's raging waters prevented him from following it.

The next explorer on the Missouri was James MacKay. MacKay was a former North West Company trader who now worked for the Spanish. MacKay traveled with John Evans, a young Welshman. They set off in 1795 and set up the trading post of Fort Charles, near present-day Homer, Nebraska. Evans continued up the Missouri and contacted the Mandan. He found that the Canadian traders were already there, so he turned back. All these journeys added significantly to the geographic knowledge of the Missouri by the end of the century.

Farther south, the Spanish city of New Orleans was also attracting U.S. traders interested in exploring the land to the west. The Irish-born Philip Nolan moved there in about 1790. He went on four journeys to trade and to explore Texas. He traveled to the Comanches and lived with them for two years. From 1794–1796 his travels took him to San Antonio. In 1797 he went to the Rio Grande and on to near present-day Austin, Texas. Nolan had become a horse trader, but the Spanish suspected him of spying. They revoked his trading license, and he was killed in a skirmish with Spanish troops. Before his death, he passed on much information about the region.

EXPLORING THE PACIFIC NORTHWEST BY SEA

Even though Americans were not exploring the Far West by land, they were going by sea. During 1787, a group of Boston merchants funded Robert Gray and John Kendrick, Boston sea captains, to take two ships to the Pacific Northwest and trade for furs. Then, they would take those furs on to China. Two years later, Gray's ship, the *Columbia*, was full and he set off for China. He left Kendrick trading on what is now Vancouver Island. Having sold his cargo in China, Gray then sailed on to Boston. Gray became the first American to circumnavigate Earth.

Gray eventually rejoined Kendrick. On May 11, 1792, he sailed south to trade and looked for shelter behind a sand bar at the mouth of a large river. He named the river Columbia after his ship. A Spaniard, Bruno de Hezeta, probably had been the first European to sight the mouth of this river in 1775. If Gray realized he was making an important discovery, his ship's log that day does not record it. It was just another day of work for Gray.

A flurry of exploring and trading activity was taking place along the Pacific Northwest coast. This increased activity attracted the attention of the Spanish, who claimed the entire region by right of discovery. Their claim almost led to war. Englishman John Meares had founded a trading post on Nootka Sound on the west coast of Vancouver Island. In 1789, he had launched the first sailing ship to be built in the region. While Meares was away, the Spanish seized his post and three of his ships. They arrested the crews. The British government made a formal protest to the Spanish. After much warlike talk, they reached an agreement in 1790. They decided to use the area jointly.

The Nootka Agreement led to another flurry of expeditions in the Far West by land and by sea. The most important of these was led by

Competition for control of the fur trade heated up when the British and the Spanish both wanted to establish trading posts on Nootka Sound on the west coast. To avoid a war, the Nootka Convention gave both countries the right to settle along the Pacific coast. Above, Nootka Sound's Friendly Cove.

British naval officer George Vancouver. The British government commissioned him to survey the coast of North America from California
to Alaska, to fill in the gaps in Captain James Cook's charts, and to
confirm—once and for all—that there was no possible northwest passage by sea. His detailed survey lasted from 1791 to 1795. His strategy
was that his large ships would anchor in a sheltered spot, while smaller
boats from his ships would go out and chart the coastline. In this way,
they charted such complex waterways as Puget Sound (where the city of
Seattle is now located) and Burrard Inlet (where the city of Vancouver
is now located).

It was a busy coastline. The Spanish were also there surveying.
José Maria Narváez was there in 1791, and Dionisio Alcala Galiano
and Cayento Valdes were there in 1792. In fact, Galiano and Valdes
met Vancouver that year and cooperated on surveying a section of the

coast together. Also in 1792 Vancouver met his Spanish counterpart, Juan Francisco Bodega y Quadra. Both commanders were experienced explorers. Bodega had been there in 1775, and Vancouver had been in the region with Cook in 1778. They each had been commissioned to meet to settle some of the remaining problems from the seizure of Meares's ships, a subject on which they could not agree. However, the two men became friendly and cooperated on their surveys. When Vancouver left the area for the winter, he went to California. His was the first non-Spanish sailing vessel to enter San Francisco Bay. He then sailed on to Monterey to meet Bodega before heading out to winter in Hawaii. Vancouver made one more survey of the coast before returning home. On that journey, he confirmed that Vancouver Island was indeed an island and concluded that there was no northwest passage.

THE FUR TRADE AT 1800

By the end of the eighteenth century, the fur trade was in trouble. Supplies of furs in the east and around the Great Lakes were exhausted. There were few animals due to overhunting. The trade depended on Native Americans. Yet, they were dying from a smallpox epidemic that swept the continent in the early 1780s. Only steady exploration into new lands kept the trade profitable.

The declining fur supply led to fierce competition between the two great British fur-trading companies, the Hudson's Bay Company and the North West Company. As each company raced to set up trading posts to cement relationships with Native American hunters, costs rose dramatically. The rivalry between the two companies was not friendly, even though prominent traders moved between the two organizations. The competition occasionally became violent, especially when rival trading posts were located near each other.

As the century came to an end, disagreements within the North West Company itself were undermining the organization. Company partners fell out over how to develop the business in the future. Some, such as Alexander Mackenzie, thought they should merge with their archrival, but few agreed. In 1798, a group of partners broke away to form a new company, popularly known as the XY Company, and in 1800 Mackenzie joined them. Although the XY Company merged back into the North West Company in 1804, this corporate turmoil reflected the tense state of the fur trade at the dawn of the nineteenth century.

Despite all of this, exploring activity continued. Peter Fidler mapped terrain in great detail, particularly in Southern Alberta. Malcolm Ross, Alexander MacKay, Duncan McGillivray, and Alexander Henry all traveled extensively along the rivers and mountains of the West through the 1790s. Between the Hudson's Bay Company, the North West Company, and independent traders, there were a large number of men whose skills led to the dramatic expansion of geographic knowledge. However, the rivalry among these firms led them to keep much of this knowledge secret.

The most active explorer of the time was David Thompson. The pace of his traveling and surveying did not let up after his great journeys earlier in the 1790s. In 1798 and 1799, he crossed the northern interior of the continent. He traveled around what is today northern Alberta and along the Saskatchewan and Churchill rivers. Thompson's career as an explorer was already remarkable, yet he was still only 30 years old. By 1812, he had logged more than 55,000 miles (88,513 km), surveying 13,000 (20,921) of them. The detailed maps he had made ranged from latitude 40°N to latitude 60°N.

Thompson's life mirrored the lives of earlier explorers. He was a careful surveyor and made his measurements as accurate as possible. He listened to those around him and learned from them. He spoke the Cree language fluently. This talent helped him negotiate and trade with Native Americans. Thompson had a wife, Charlotte Small, who was the daughter of a British partner in the North West Company and a Cree woman. Thompson married Charlotte in a civil ceremony in summer 1799. The two were together until their deaths more than 57 years later.

The fur trade offered men many opportunities. For a few there were fortunes to be made. Thompson and Mackenzie, for example, became rich. For many other men, the trade offered a steady job. The job was a difficult one. However, it offered freedom from supervision.

NATIVE PEOPLES AND EXPLORATION

Many journeys of exploration depended on native people. Often the guides discovered portages linking rivers. They led explorers to well-worn native routes along which there were already long-standing networks of trade. Native American leadership, language, and diplomatic skills were essential to an expedition's success. Additionally, European explorers were generally unprepared for the hard life of northeastern North America. They needed assistance to cope with it. This was a role particularly played by Native American women. They married fur traders as part of diplomatic and commercial ties. These marriages introduced traders to the customs of the region.

Native American trade networks tended to be local, that is, with people with whom they had direct contact. Trade items passed along a

AFRICAN AMERICANS IN THE FUR TRADE

One group who found greater freedom in the West were the few people of African descent who worked in the fur trade. Africans, free and enslaved, had been part of the fur trade since settlers had arrived in North America. One of the first was Mattias de Sousa, who had arrived in North America as an indentured servant—that is, someone who agreed to labor for a set period (usually five years) in exchange for his or her passage, food, and shelter. When Sousa's servitude was over, he had traded furs on Chesapeake Bay in the 1640s. Jean-Baptiste Pointe du Sable, a free man who was born in Haiti in the Caribbean and was the son of an African slave mother and a French father, arrived in New Orleans in 1779. He entered the fur trade and lived for 16 years at the mouth of the Chicago River on Lake Michigan. As had other French fur traders, he married a Potawatomi woman named Catherine, and together they ran a trading post for many years. Although slave labor was more commonly used on plantations, a few slaves found themselves in the fur trade. Pierre Bonga was owned by a North West Company trader and was frequently left to run the post while his master was gone on long journeys. Bonga became a skilled linguist, and married a Chippewa woman, and, since the status of children followed from the mother, their children were free. As the nineteenth century dawned, the fur trade in the Far West offered opportunities for many people from many walks of life.

chain of trading relationships. Europeans created a larger market and connected Native Peoples to a global network. In doing so, Native diplomatic and military relationships were changed, as nations in strategic locations were able to exploit their position and become middlemen. This is what the Cree did between Native communities in the Far West and the Hudson's Bay Company.

The arrival of Europeans transformed the landscape in other profound ways. The Europeans cleared forests for agriculture. They introduced plants and animals that often devastated local species. Most important, they introduced new diseases to which the Native Peoples had no resistance. Many became sick and died, resulting in catastrophic population decline. To survive, communities merged. As a result, languages and cultures were lost.

Europeans brought other kinds of change to Native Peoples. Hunting became a year-round activity instead of a seasonal one. Communities became dependent on trade goods such as firearms, kettles, and cloth. Military alliances shifted. European power struggles had a direct impact on the Native world. At the end of the eighteenth century, Native Peoples had to continue to face the ambitions of European powers and the new United States of America. With the rapidly growing population of the United States, settlers already were farming in what had recently been Native American land west of the Appalachians, and some of its citizens already were looking to discover more of the resources of the Far West.

THE UNITED STATES LOOKS WEST

European powers had long searched for a northwest passage across North America. Some in the United States shared that goal. In 1792, U.S. captain Robert Gray had found the mouth of the Columbia River. Traders felt that this might be the route to the Pacific they had been searching for. They just needed to find it inland. Alexander Mackenzie, on his 1793 expedition, thought he had briefly been on it before turbulent waters drove him to seek a more navigable route. In fact, he had been on the Fraser River. So, while Mackenzie had reached the Pacific, he had not found an easily navigable trade route, and explorers still searched for the Columbia River.

The search would be completed early in the next century. It would be the 1804–1806 journey of a U.S. government-sponsored expedition led by Meriwether Lewis and William Clark that located the Columbia by an inland route. It would be five years after that, in 1811, before David Thompson would lead a party that traveled the length of the river to the Pacific. Gray, Lewis and Clark, and Thompson had found a great river to the Pacific, but not an easily navigable one. There was no equivalent of the Mississippi that would provide easy access to the Pacific. Although San Francisco had been founded as early as 1776, it would be some time before dynamic commercial cities such as New Orleans and St. Louis— neither of which belonged to the United States in 1800—would appear in the land west of the Mississippi.

Such developments lay in the future. At the end of the eighteenth century, Thomas Jefferson was among those Americans intrigued by the opportunities of the West. He had written the first of the Northwest Ordinances of the 1780s. These acts laid out the way in which territories would be admitted to the Union.

Thomas Jefferson believed that the growth of the country would come from widespread property ownership. The Northwest Ordinance, passed in 1787, created a policy that increased the westward expansion of the United States by allowing unclaimed land to be sold to settlers and speculators. Above, a century after the first Northwest Ordinance, a family poses in front of their wagon in Loup Valley, Nebraska, on their way to their new homestead in the West.

Part of Jefferson's interest in exploration was linked to his political philosophy, in which he thought that the nation's security would come from widespread property ownership. At the time, in most states, only white men who owned property could vote. To Jefferson, more property owners meant more men who would have a stake in the future of the country and the government. He hoped for a nation of small, independent farmers. That vision of the future required land, and he saw the territory to the west of the Appalachians and east of the Mississippi as available to fulfill that vision. The Northwest Ordinances and the later Southwest Ordinance of 1790 laid out plans for mapping the territory, surveying the land, and selling it off to settlers and speculators. (The "Northwest" and "Southwest" referred at the time to land east of the Mississippi.)

THE END OF A QUEST

For 300 years, European explorers had searched for a northwest passage to Asia. Their quest led them from the Arctic Circle all the way to Florida. From there, they headed inland across North America, steadily moving farther west by rivers and lakes, until they were finally successful in finding the last piece of the puzzle, a river that led to the Pacific. There had been many failures along the way. When there were great successes, they often involved strong leadership, good planning, skilled teams or crews, active cooperation of Native Peoples, and a good deal of luck.

The eighteenth century ended with great journeys of exploration. They altered and clarified the map of North America. The dream of an ocean northwest passage was halted. In its place came a vast array of knowledge about the Pacific Northwest. Many of the great waterways of the continent were mapped. Trade and international rivalry still drove exploring activities. Many U.S. traders and adventurers believed that there were more rivers and many more riches to be found in the West. The century to follow would prove them right.

By the end of the eighteenth century, the new United States—now proudly building its capital in Washington, D.C.—joined European powers in staking a claim to North American territory. It was entirely uncertain who would control the continent as the nineteenth century dawned. Geographic knowledge would be as critical in the nineteenth century as it had been in the earlier years. Discovery and exploration would continue to determine the future of North America.

Chronology

1496	King Henry VII orders scribes to draft letters patent, granting exclusive British rights to conquer and trade with any newly discovered land.
1497	John Cabot lands in North America on June 24. This is the first recorded voyage to do so since the Vikings.
ca. 1504	First known voyages of the French to Newfoundland take place.
1513	Vasco Núñez de Balboa crosses the Isthmus of Panama.
	◆ Spain claims Florida and installs Juan Ponce de León as governor.
1516	Peter Martyr's *Decades of the New World* (*De orbe novo decades*) supplies evidence that waters flow from Asia to the Atlantic.
1524	Giovanni da Verrazano sails to America in search of a passageway to China. He lands somewhere near Cape Fear at the lowest-point of present-day North Carolina. He also reaches New York Harbor (naming it Land of Angoulême), Block Island (which he called Aloysia), and Rhode Island (named after the island of Rhodes).
1534	On his first voyage, Jacques Cartier explores parts of Newfoundland, areas of the Canadian Atlantic provinces, and the Gulf of St. Lawrence. He kidnaps Chief Donnacona's sons and returns to France with them.
1535–1536	On his second voyage, Cartier becomes the first European to sail up the St. Lawrence River. Donnacona is reunited with his sons. Cartier returns to France with Donnacona, Donnacona's sons, and children he had been given as presents.

1539	Hernando de Soto lands in Tampa Bay, Florida, then explores Florida's west coast.
1540–1541	De Soto explores Georgia, South Carolina, North Carolina, Tennessee, Alabama, Mississippi, then travels west through Arkansas, Oklahoma, Louisiana, and Texas. His expedition is the first to document seeing the Mississippi River.
1541–1542	On his third voyage, Cartier builds a settlement called Charlesbourg-Royal in present-day Quebec.
1585–1590	Sir Walter Raleigh's attempts to colonize a region of North America called Roanoke Island (present-day states of North Carolina and Virginia) ends in failure. He does pave the way for future colonies.

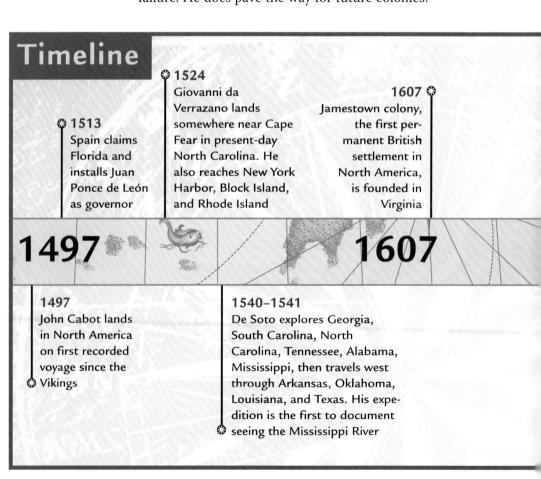

Timeline

1524
Giovanni da Verrazano lands somewhere near Cape Fear in present-day North Carolina. He also reaches New York Harbor, Block Island, and Rhode Island

1513
Spain claims Florida and installs Juan Ponce de León as governor

1607
Jamestown colony, the first permanent British settlement in North America, is founded in Virginia

1497

1607

1497
John Cabot lands in North America on first recorded voyage since the Vikings

1540–1541
De Soto explores Georgia, South Carolina, North Carolina, Tennessee, Alabama, Mississippi, then travels west through Arkansas, Oklahoma, Louisiana, and Texas. His expedition is the first to document seeing the Mississippi River

1607	Jamestown colony, the first permanent British settlement in North America, is founded in Virginia.
1608	Samuel de Champlain establishes the first permanent French settlement in present-day Quebec.
1670	The Hudson's Bay Company is created by royal charter. It is granted a monopoly over the fur trade and the right to govern Hudson's Bay and the land draining into it (more than 3 million miles, or 4.8 million kilometers).
1673	Father Jacques Marquette and Louis Jolliet lead a party from Lake Michigan all the way to the Mississippi River. They decide to turn back before reaching the Gulf of Mexico.

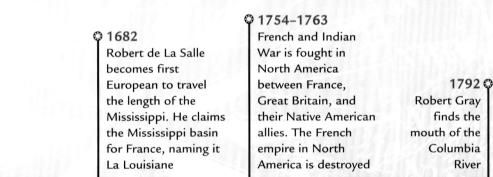

✺ **1682**
Robert de La Salle becomes first European to travel the length of the Mississippi. He claims the Mississippi basin for France, naming it La Louisiane

✺ **1754–1763**
French and Indian War is fought in North America between France, Great Britain, and their Native American allies. The French empire in North America is destroyed

1792 ✺
Robert Gray finds the mouth of the Columbia River

1670

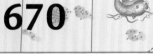

1793

1670
The Hudson's Bay Company is granted a monopoly over the fur trade and the right to govern Hudson's Bay and the land draining into it (more than ✺ 3 million miles)

1783
The North West Company is formed to compete with the Hudson's Bay Company in the fur trade ✺ business

1793
Alexander Mackenzie finds route across North America in its northern latitudes, crossing the Continental Divide ✺

1679	Robert de La Salle and crew, including Father Louis Hennepin, sail on the *Griffon*, the first ship to navigate the Great Lakes.
1681	William Penn obtains permission to establish a colony in Pennsylvania. The European population in North America soars to almost 20,000 within 20 years.
1682	Robert de La Salle sails down the Mississippi all the way to the Gulf of Mexico, becoming the first European to travel the length of the Mississippi. He claims the Mississippi basin for France, naming it La Louisiane.
1743	Sons of Pierre La Vérendrye claim today's Pierre, South Dakota, for France.
1754–1763	French and Indian War is fought in North America between France, Great Britain, and their Native American allies, for control of the Forks of the Ohio River (present-day Pittsburgh). The French empire in North America is destroyed.
1783	The North West Company is formed to compete with the Hudson's Bay Company in the fur trade business.
1792	Robert Gray finds the mouth of the Columbia River. David Thompson later travels the river to the Pacific Ocean.
1793	After several attempts, Alexander Mackenzie finds route across North America in its northern latitudes, crossing the Continental Divide.

Glossary

America—This term, which only gradually supplanted the name New World, was created in 1507 by obscure German mapmaker Martin Waldseemüller to match the other feminine names of continents (Europa, Africa, and Asia). It was created from the name of Florentine explorer Amerigo Vespucci, who claimed to have been the first European to set foot on the continent.

astrolabe—A metal disc that hangs from a frame; precisely measured marks and grooves allow the navigator to sight stars or the sun and determine the degrees of elevation. From ancient times on, it was used in navigation, along with charts accounting for seasonal variation. Mariners could thus figure out where they were north or south on Earth (latitude), but it would be the eighteenth century before other instruments allowed them to determine their location east or west (longitude). The astrolabe itself was replaced by more modern instruments, such as the sextant.

Bretons—A Celtic people from the far northwest coast of France in the province of Brittany. This region was only incorporated into France in the sixteenth century and kept its own language and culture as well as its seafaring traditions. Bretons were long involved in North Atlantic fishing.

cannibalism—Derived from the early Spaniards' pronunciation of the Carib people—from which the Caribbean Sea also takes its name—the eating of human flesh. In fact, few native peoples on the North American continent practiced it, and ironically it is among desperate starving Europeans that the practice is recorded most frequently.

cartographer—A maker of maps or charts.

cod—A species of fish found in abundance in the North Atlantic, usually salted as bacalao or dried as stockfish, and in great demand in Europe, particularly in Catholic countries, where dietary restrictions during Lent and every Friday forbid eating of meat or animal products.

colony—A territorial possession permanently occupied by settlers and ruled directly by the mother country or indirectly by appointed officials. Colonies usually were exploited for their natural resources or commercially grown crops. They provided a market for European goods and could be used as a base for trade.

coureurs de bois—French phrase literally meaning "runners of the woods." Coureurs de bois was the name given to independent French fur traders who went into the interior of the country to trade. Since there was an official trading monopoly early in the history of New France, these men were outlaws, so the term was not a compliment. Later, when there was no longer a trading monopoly, it was simply descriptive.

Covenant Chain—A metaphor for the various councils and treaties intended to maintain good relations between the Iroquois and various European settlers—Dutch, English, and French. The Iroquois themselves used the term and were alleged to have a wampum (bead) belt that portrayed this relationship by two boats symbolizing the two peoples moving along separately but in peace. The English in particular tried to exploit this "covenant" by supporting and encouraging the Iroquois to dominate other Native Americans in the Northeast and thereby gaining security that allowed for economic growth.

dyewood—A number of plants and exotic woods used to dye cloth. Although no major source of these was found in North America, it was often a stated objective of explorers to find such dyes and to provide competition for the very lucrative trade in Brazil wood from South America.

empire—A series of colonies, trading posts, or subject states held by a nation-state or sometimes a corporate body and usually ruled over by the mother country. The term refers to the total sum of such holdings. It often assumes a policy for governing or exploiting such possessions in the interest of the mother country and often to the detriment of the Native populations.

fool's gold—Technically, iron pyrite, a mineral with a brass coloring that has often led people to believe they have found ore with gold.

galley—A long flat ship powered by either sail or oar typically used in Mediterranean trade and often manned by captive slaves taken in combat or by prisoners. The term later came to refer to the kitchen facilities on a ship.

Great Khan—The emperor of China whom many early explorers hoped to meet at the end of their journey. The term is of Turkic origin, and Europeans probably learned it from Marco Polo, who claimed to have visited China during the Yuan dynasty when Mongols ruled China. The emperors of the Ming dynasty (1368–1644), the period of the search for a route to China, would not have used the term.

indentured servant—An individual who has agreed to give his or her labor for a number of years, at the end of which time the individual is granted freedom. In the case of the early period of colonization of North America, indentured servants usually were bound for about five years in exchange for passage to North America and food and board for the period of service.

inland northwest passage—A river that Europeans hoped to find that would allow them to navigate across the North American continent easily and would allow traders to travel from the Atlantic to the Pacific Ocean.

intendant—A powerful official in New France responsible for the administration of justice and economic growth.

isthmus—A narrow neck of land that connects two larger bodies of land.

Jesuits—Formally called the Society of Jesus; a religious order of the Catholic Church founded by Ignatius of Loyola in 1534. The order had, and still has, educational and scientific interests in addition to its missionary work.

joint-stock company—A financial innovation of the seventeenth century; usually a temporary association of investors, each of whom owned a certain number of shares or percentage of a specified venture. Eventually, these stocks became negotiable and could be traded as they are today in the stock exchange.

league—A measure of length of distance that varies considerably in different times and in different countries and based on whether the measure is on land or sea. It is usually the equivalent of about two and a half to three miles as a land measure, and three to four and a half miles as a sea measure.

letters patent—During the European age of exploration, an official decree whereby an individual was granted exclusive rights
to explore and exploit a region for a specified number of years.
As with a modern patent on an invention or a copyright, it was
assumed that the person who bore the expense and whose ideas
led to the discovery should be allowed to reap a profit from it
without competition.

Loyalists—North American colonists who stayed loyal to the British
during the American Revolution. Many of them left the United
States during and after the war and went to live in Canada, particularly Upper Canada (now Ontario), Nova Scotia, and New
Brunswick. Others went to live in England.

mercantile empire—A series of overseas possessions strung into a
network of fortified posts specifically designed to facilitate and
protect trade. These usually were maintained by the state as an
object of national interest rather than by private investors. These
are contrasted by colonial empires, in which entire regions are
held and occupied by settlers.

monopoly—More or less total control over the production and trade
of certain products or services. Early modern states often granted
exclusive rights to an individual or company to trade or produce
a certain commodity. A monopoly to explore a certain region, to
import fish, or even to produce simple things like soap could be
enormously lucrative. The economic benefit, so theorists believed,
was that, with such total control, a business was guaranteed success, with which it could compete with foreign businesses and
thus bring money into the country. Unlike today, monopolies were
not seen as stifling healthy competition and free trade.

nation-state—An area of land that is ruled by one centralized
administration; in the early modern period this was usually by a
royal dynasty. The nation-state is also assumed to have a common culture, language, and often ethnic unity that distinguishes it
from other nations, though this often has meant ignoring or con-
sciously effacing local identities.

nobles—A hereditary and titled aristocratic class in European society
that often served military or administrative functions. In some
countries, such as France and Spain, nobles were exempt from

paying taxes. The base of their power was landholding, so acquiring estates in the New World was a major reason they became investors in overseas exploration.

Normans—Derived from the word "Northmen," a reference to their ancestors, the Vikings, who settled in France. These people from the north coast of France—what became known as the province of Normandy—were expert seamen and became active early in fishing North Atlantic waters.

Northwest Passage—The sea route to Asia via a strait believed to exist cutting across the North American continent, but in fact the actual passage requires an extremely difficult journey through frozen and iceberg-laden waters some 500 miles above the Arctic Circle in what is now the Northwest Territories of Canada and above Alaska.

peddler—This is a general term describing people who go from place to place buying and selling (peddling) goods. It was specifically used by the Hudson's Bay Company to describe traders from the North West Company in order to belittle them.

Pilgrims—A term adopted by the radical Protestant settlers aboard the Mayflower who landed in Massachusetts in 1620. The generic (lowercased) form of the term originally is derived from a person who makes a journey, known as a pilgrimage, to a holy site where a miracle had occurred, such as Rome, Jerusalem, or Mecca.

plantation—Although originally referring to any colonial settlement, it eventually came to mean a large estate producing a commercial crop for export, such as tobacco or cotton, and worked by slave labor.

portage—This French word, now also used in English, refers both to the act of carrying canoes and all supplies around an obstacle, such as rapids or a waterfall on a river, and to the places and routes where such an act is required.

portolan chart—From the Latin for "port" or "harbor," charts indicating the distances between ports and along coastlines. These charts directly preceded and contributed to the mapmaking techniques in the age of exploration.

privateering—An official license to seize plunder from enemy ships, which in practice differed little from acts of piracy. European rulers found this an effective way to strike their opponents without having to spend money, and for investors it could mean good profits despite the decline in trade caused by war.

Proclamation Line—This was the name given to a British royal proclamation of 1763 that restricted British colonists in North America from settling west of the Appalachians. The goal was to slow down settlement in the West while British authorities negotiated and purchased Native American lands. The colonists almost immediately disregarded this proclamation.

Protestant—A follower of any one of the churches that had "protested" against and broken away from the Roman Catholic Church in the sixteenth century. These include German Lutherans; the Swiss, Dutch, and Scottish Reformed Churches; the French Huguenots; as well as the Church of England. Religion became a major point of conflict among nations involved in exploration.

Puritan—A term (based on "purify") denoting a Protestant who sought further and more thorough reform of the Church of England, usually along lines specified by French theologian Jean Calvin. The majority of settlers to the Massachusetts Bay colony and New England in the seventeenth century were Puritans.

scurvy—A potentially fatal illness resulting from a deficiency of vitamin C. Its symptoms include bleeding gums and swollen limbs. The human body can obtain sufficient vitamin C from many foods, but sailors who spent many months at sea with a limited diet were at high risk to get scurvy. It could be cured with citrus juice or with a liquid made by boiling spruce or arborvitae (an evergreen shrub).

slavery—Keeping people in servitude and as property. Technically, Europeans would only make slaves out of captives taken in battle. In fact, they often initiated warfare in order to justify taking slaves. In the case of Africa, they often bought slaves from Africans who had captured them. The Spanish enslaved many Native Americans in their New World territories. In North America, Native populations were rarely reduced to slavery because traders and colonists depended on them, but in the plantation economy of the South, African slaves comprised an overwhelming proportion of the labor force.

spices—A culinary rather than strict botanical term, spices refer to the dried bark, root, fruit, bud, or other part of usually tropical plants imported by Europeans and sold at enormous profit. Among those most in demand were pepper, cloves, nutmeg, and cinnamon from Southeast Asia.

Sulpicians—A religious order established in 1642 by Abbé Olier of the parish of St. Sulpice in France. The order trained men for the priesthood.

Treaty of Tordesillas—Named after the city in Spain where in 1494 an agreement was made between Spain and Portugal and given assent by Pope Alexander VI, dividing the entire world into two halves along a line 370 leagues west of the Cape Verde Islands—about 48° west of the Greenwich (Prime) meridian. Spain would have the right to explore and conquer most of the New World; Portugal was given Africa and Asia, and as it turned out Brazil and a claim to Newfoundland as well. These terms became impossible to enforce once other European powers actively engaged in exploration, particularly in North America.

West Indies—Due to a geographical misconception, the Caribbean was thought to be adjacent to South Asia, or the "East Indies," and so was regarded as the West Indies. As a result, the term for all Native Americans was "Indians."

Bibliography

Armstrong, Joe C. *Champlain*. Toronto: Macmillan of Canada, 1987.

Axtell, James. *Beyond 1492: Encounters in Colonial North America*. New York: Oxford University Press, 1992.

———. *The Invasion Within: The Contest of Cultures in Colonial North America*. New York: Oxford University Press, 1985.

Boucher, Philip P. *Les Nouvelles Frances: France in America, 1500–1815, An Imperial Perspective*. Providence, R.I.: John Carter Brown Library, 1989.

Buisseret, David. *Mapping the French Empire in North America*. Chicago: Newberry Library, 1991.

Calloway, Colin. *First Peoples: A Documentary Survey of American Indian History*. New York: Bedford St. Martin's, 1999.

———. *New Worlds for All: Indians, Europeans, and the Remaking of Early America*. Baltimore: Johns Hopkins University Press, 1997.

Cartier, Jacques. *The Voyages of Jacques Cartier*. Toronto: University of Toronto Press, 1993.

Cavan, Seamus. *Daniel Boone and the Opening of the Ohio Country*. New York: Chelsea House Publishers, 1991.

Codignola, Luca. "Another Look at Verrazzano's Voyage, 1524." *Acadiensis* vol. 29, no. 1, 1999: 29–42.

De Vorsey, Louis, et al. *Columbus and the Land of Ayllón: The Exploration and Settlement of the Southeast*. Valona, Ga.: Lower Altamaha Historical Society, 1992.

Durant, David N. *Raleigh's Lost Colony*. New York: Atheneum, 1981.

Eckert, Allan W. *That Dark and Bloody River: Chronicles of the Ohio River Valley*. New York: Bantam Books, 1995.

Emerson, Everett H. *Captain John Smith*. New York: Maxwell Macmillan International, 1993.

Faragher, John Mack. *Daniel Boone: The Life and Legend of an American Pioneer*. New York: Henry Holt & Co., 1992.

Fenn, Elizabeth. *Pox Americana: The Great Smallpox Epidemic of 1775–82*. New York: Hill and Wang, 2002.

Firstbrook, P. L. *The Voyage of the Matthew: John Cabot and the Discovery of North America*. London: BBC Books, 1997.

Gleach, Frederic W. *Powhattan's World and Colonial Virginia*. Lincoln: University of Nebraska Press, 1997.

Gough, Barry. *First Across the Continent: Sir Alexander Mackenzie*. The Oklahoma Western Biographies, Vol. 14. Norman, Okla.: University of Oklahoma Press, 1997.

Greer, Allan. *The Jesuit Relations: Natives and Missionaries in Seventeenth-Century North America*. New York: Bedford/St. Martins, 2000.

Hudson, Charles M. *The Juan Pardo Expeditions: Exploration of the Carolinas and Tennessee, 1566–1568*. Transcribed, translated, and annotated by Paul E. Hoffman. Washington, D.C.: Smithsonian Institution Press, 1990.

Johnson, Donald S. *Charting the Sea of Darkness: The Four Voyages of Henry Hudson*. Camden, Me.: International Marine, 1993.

Jones, Phil. *Raleigh's Pirate Colony in America: The Lost Settlement of Roanake 1584–1590*. Charleston, S.C.: Tempus, 2001.

Joutel, Henri. *The La Salle Expedition to Texas: The Journal of Henri Joutel, 1684–1687*. Edited by William C. Foster; translated by Johanna S. Warren. Austin: Texas State Historical Association, 1998.

Kupperman, Karen Ordahl. *Indians and English: Facing off in Early America*. Ithaca, N.Y.: Cornell University Press, 2000.

———. "Roanoke Lost" *American Heritage*, vol. 36, no. 5, 1985: pp. 81–96.

Lemay, J. A. Leo. *The American Dream of Captain John Smith*. Charlottesville: University Press of Virginia, 1991.

Lyon, Eugene. *The Enterprise of Florida: Pedro Menéndez de Avilés and the Spanish Conquest of 1565–1568*. Gainesville: University Presses of Florida, 1976.

———. *Pedro Menéndez de Avilés*. New York: Garland, 1995.

McConnell, Michael N. *A Country Between: The Upper Ohio River Valley and Its Peoples, 1724–1774*. Lincoln: University of Nebraska Press, 1992.

Morison, Samuel Eliot. *The European Discovery of America: The Northern Voyages*. New York: Oxford University Press, 1971.

Namias, June. *White Captives: Gender and Ethnicity on the American Frontier*. Chapel Hill: University of North Carolina Press, 1993.

Pope, Peter Edward. *The Many Landfalls of John Cabot*. Toronto: University of Toronto Press, 1997.

Richter, Daniel K. *Facing East from Indian Country: A Native History of Early America*. Cambridge: Cambridge University Press, 2003.

Shirley, John William. *Thomas Harriot, a Biography*. New York: Oxford University Press, 1983.

Sinclair, Andrew. *Sir Walter Raleigh and the Age of Discovery*. Harmondsworth, New York: Penguin, 1984.

Stannard, David. *American Holocaust: The Conquest of the New World*. New York: Oxford University Press, 1992.

Swagerty, William R. "Indian Trade in the Trans-Mississippi West to 1870." *The Handbook of North American Indians* Vol. 4, History of Indian White Relations. Edited by William E. Washburn. Washington, D.C.: Smithsonian Institution Press, 1988, pp. 351–374.

Usner, Daniel H. *Indians, Settlers, and Slaves in a Frontier Exchange Economy: The Lower Mississippi Valley Before 1783.* Chapel Hill: University of North Carolina Press, 1992.

Van Kirk, Sylvia. *Many Tender Ties: Women in Fur Trade Society, 1670–1870.* Norman: University of Oklahoma Press, 1980.

White, Richard. *The Middle Ground: Indians, Empires, and Republics in the Great Lakes Region, 1650–1815.* Cambridge: Cambridge University Press, 1991.

Winsor, Justin, and George E. Ellis. *Early Spanish, French, and English Encounters with American Indians.* Edited by Anne Paolucci and Henry Paolucci. Whitestone, N.Y.: Council on National Literatures, 1997.

Wroth, Lawrence C. *The Voyages of Giovanni da Verrazzano, 1524–1528.* New Haven, Conn.: Yale University Press, 1970.

Further Resources

FICTION

Aaseng, Nathan. *You Are the Explorer*. Minneapolis: Oliver Press Inc., 2000.

Cooper, James Fenimore. *The Deerslayer*. New York: Bantam, Doubleday, Dell, 1982.

———. *The Last of the Mohicans*. New York: Barnes & Noble Books, 2003.

———. *The Pathfinder*. New York: Signet Classics, 1976.

Garfield, Henry. *The Lost Voyage of John Cabot*. New York: Simon & Schuster, 2004.

Hesse, Karen. *Stowaway*. New York: Margaret McElderry Books, 2000.

Manson, Ainslie. *A Dog Came, Too: A True Story*. New York: Margaret McElderry Books, 1993.

Moore, Brian. *Black Robe*. New York: Plume Reprint, 1997.

Speare, Elizabeth George. *The Sign of the Beaver*. New York: Houghton Mifflin, 1984.

Stainer, M. L. *The Lyon's Roar*. Circleville, N.Y.: Chicken Soup Press, 1999.

VHS/DVD

Black Robe (1991). MGM, DVD/VHS, 2001.

Cabot (1997). Bristol Film and Video Society, VHS, 1997.

Canada: A People's History (2000). Canadian Broadcasting Corporation, DVD/VHS, 2000.

Empire by the Bay: Ambition, Wealth, and the Hudson's Bay Company (2000). PBS Video, VHS, 2000.

Golden Age of Exploration (1997). Knowledge Unlimited, VHS, 1997.

Last of the Mohicans (1992). Twentieth Century Fox, DVD/VHS, 2001.

Lost Colony of Roanoke (1999). A&E Home Videos, VHS, 2000.

The Mayflower Pilgrims (1996). Janson Video, VHS, 1996.

WEB SITES

Avalon Project at Yale Law School: The Letters Patents of King Henry the Seventh Granted unto Iohn Cabot and his Three Sonnes, Lewis, Sebastian and Sancius for the Discouerie of New and Unknowen Lands

http://www.yale.edu/lawweb/avalon/cabot01.htm

The original text from the letters patent that granted John Cabot and his sons the right to discover unknown lands in the New World.

Canadian Museum of Civilization
http://www.civilisations.ca/cmc/home/cmc-home

Exhibits, programs, events supported by the Canadian Museum. Includes the Virtual Museum of New France, which details French exploration in North America.

Enchanted Learning: Explorers of North and Central America
http://www.enchantedlearning.com/explorers/namerica.shtml

Biographies of great explorers of North and Central America.

Fort Raleigh National Historic Site
http://www.nps.gov/fora/forteachers/roanoke-revisited.htm

The National Park Service site about England's first home in the New World. Includes Roanoke Revisited, supplemental materials for students and teachers about the Lost Colony, the failed colony of Walter Raleigh.

Giovanni da Verrazzano
http://www.win.tue.nl/~engels/discovery/ verrazzano.html

The biography of Giovanni da Verrazzano, the founder of New York Harbor.

Jacques Cartier, Explorer
http://www.publicbookshelf.com/public_html/Our_Country_Vol_1/jacquesca_cd.html

The biography of Jacques Cartier, from an excerpt from volume one of Our Country, published in the late 1800s. The series chronicles American history from Viking exploration through the French and Indian Wars.

The Lost Colony Productions
http://www.thelostcolony.org/index.htm

In its seventy-second season, this is a live production about the history of the Lost Colony of Roanoke.

PBS: Empire of the Bay—Alexander Mackenzie
http://www.pbs.org/empireofthebay/profiles/mackenzie.html

The biography of the first European north of Mexico to reach the Pacific Ocean on an overland route.

Picture Credits

Index

About the Contributors

Author **CAROLINE COX** holds an A.B., an M.A., and a Ph.D., all in history, from the University of California at Berkeley. She is an associate professor of history at the University of the Pacific. Author of a book on the American Revolution and articles and book reviews focused on American history, Cox has taught courses on subjects ranging from colonial and revolutionary America to American cultures and U.S. military history.

Author **KEN ALBALA** holds a B.A. in early modern European studies from George Washington University, an M.A. in history from Yale University, and a Ph.D. in history from Columbia University. Albala is an associate professor and chair of the history department of the University of the Pacific. He is the author of three books and more than 15 book chapters and articles, specializing in the history of food.

General editor **JOHN S. BOWMAN** received a B.A. in English literature from Harvard University and matriculated at Trinity College, Cambridge University, as Harvard's Fiske Scholar and at the University of Munich. Bowman has worked as an editor and as a freelance writer for more than 40 years. He has edited numerous works of history, as well as served as general editor of Chelsea House's AMERICA AT WAR set. Bowman is the author of more than 10 books, including a volume in this series, *Exploration in the World of the Ancients, Revised Edition.*

General editor **MAURICE ISSERMAN** holds a B.A. in history from Reed College and an M.A. and Ph.D. in history from the University of Rochester. He is a professor of history at Hamilton College, specializing in twentieth-century U.S. history and the history of exploration. Isserman was a Fulbright distinguished lecturer at Moscow State University. He is the author of 12 books.